# THE A-Z OF CURIOUS
# ABERDEENSHIRE

## STRANGE STORIES OF MYSTERIES, CRIMES AND ECCENTRICS

DUNCAN HARLEY

The History Press

*Ivor Cutler once commented that the imperfections*
*of life can often be achingly moving.*

First published 2017
Reprinted 2018

The History Press
The Mill, Brimscombe Port
Stroud, Gloucestershire, GL5 2QG
www.thehistorypress.co.uk

British Library Cataloguing in Publication Data.
A catalogue record for this book is available from the British Library.

ISBN 978 0 7509 8379 2

Typesetting and origination by The History Press
Printed in Great Britain

# Contents

Acknowledgements                     5

Introduction                         7


*The A-Z of Curious Aberdeenshire*   9


About the Author                   160

# Acknowledgements

Everyone should write a book at least once in their lifetime and I count myself one of the lucky few who have made it into print. Friends and colleagues along the way have contributed ideas for stories, and relationships past and present have enabled it to happen. In particular, I would like to thank Nigel Lucas, who showed me the value of being inquisitive. He is no longer around, but is well missed.

Judy Mackie, editor of *Leopard Magazine*, and that stalwart of the *Northern Scot*, Mike Collins, have encouraged my writing and, indeed, have often funded it. Mike freely gave me a platform and when, on occasion, he was unable to use my stories, willingly passed them on to others for publication. As for Judy, she must have often wondered what on earth I would send her next. From early beginnings as an occasional contributor to *Leopard* she quickly promoted me to the status of regular columnist. Over the course of an apprenticeship of several years she both edited my work and encouraged me to explore Aberdeenshire with an open mind and often with an open chequebook. The Our Town series was the result and what an eye-opener it was. From Portsoy in the north to Stonehaven in the south, no town in the north-east of Scotland was safe from *Leopard*'s scrutiny.

*Aberdeen Voice* also deserves special recognition. As a not-for-profit weekly publication it has, to the best of my knowledge, published more or less anything I have ever submitted. Special thanks are due to editor Fred Wilkinson and *Voice* sub-editor Paul Kohn.

I am also grateful to the family of the late great Doric poet Bob Smith for their open invitation to include his work. He and I collaborated several times before his demise. In 2014 I had penned an article about a celebrated Aberdeenshire cow for the *Scottish Review* and Bob's 'Turra Coo' accompanied the piece. As a tribute to the man, I have included his poem here in its entirety in the section helpfully entitled 'Cattle'.

The various local newspapers or *squeaks* encountered along the way have also been well appreciated. There will, I hope, be better days ahead for weekly local journalism.

My companion Janice Rayne has always encouraged the writing, often at great personal sacrifice and I am grateful for her support in the making of this book. She and I have had many adventures along the way. My lifelong pal James Bryce also deserves special thanks. He has always encouraged my writing on the basis that anyone who owns a pen can write a book. I only hope that he is correct in his assumption.

A very few of the stories within have been published in one form or another across the years and in this volume I have enhanced and in most cases completely rewritten such pieces in the hope of securing appreciation from a new audience. As far as I can tell, most of what follows is completely true but please forgive those infamous last words.

I hope you enjoy *The A–Z of Curious Aberdeenshire*. It's been a good few years in the making.

# Introduction

The folklore and the history of Aberdeenshire make for interesting reading. Invading armies have come and gone and the boom and bust of oil has changed the landscape forever. Where bloody battles were won and lost, gas pipelines and shiny white windmills now litter the landscape.

Along the way the Romans left their mark and evidence, in the form of long-abandoned marching camps, is still being excavated. The Picts, for their part, left a more obvious heritage in the form of symbol stones and hill forts. Macbeth, Burns and Inkson McConnochie all played their part in shaping the folklore of the North-east, and the monarchs and the lairds, for their part, often took more decisive action. As a sometimes-tearful populace looked on, they variously managed the land and, more often than not, plundered it mercilessly. Mary Queen of Scots, the doomed Marquis of Montrose and those Jacobite Pretenders ravished the landscape and, in consequence, often exposed the population to the full horrors of civil war and state-sponsored vengeance. The castles of old bear witness to the cruelty of the past and the ballads of old record the tumultuous events that shaped the history of the north-east of Scotland.

Inevitably in a work of this kind there will be a few 'floating' folk tales that readers may recognise as belonging elsewhere. Secret tunnels and bottomless pools are typical of the genre. I make no apology for including these and will leave it to the reader to judge their accuracy.

*The A–Z of Curious Aberdeenshire* is a varied collection of tales intended both to satisfy the casual reader and hopefully act as a primer for those, both tourists and locals, who yearn to learn more about the people and the events that have shaped this beautiful part of Scotland.

I hope that these wee snippets of history will both satisfy and enthral the reader. Please dip in to these pages and smile gently at the past.

Note: The terms Aberdeenshire, the North-east and Grampian are variously used to refer to the County of Aberdeenshire.

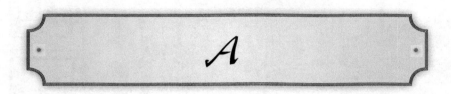

### ❧ ABERDEENSHIRE ART ❧

The landscape of Aberdeenshire is littered with structures as old as the pyramids of both Egypt and Peru, and most settlements in the county can boast a standing stone or two. Many are host to stone circles rivalling Stonehenge and a select few are home to ancient artefacts in the shape of 4,000-year-old carved stone balls. Known as 'petrospheres' and dating from Neolithic times, these are typically 7cm across with between three and 160 protruding knobs on their surface. They could be weapons, coinage, loom weights or religious objects. No one really knows for sure.

Scotland currently boasts two public art installations based on these mysterious objects. Festival Square in the very heart of Edinburgh's financial district features First Conundrum, created for the millennium celebrations by artist Remco de Fouw, which consists of a series of Neolithic carved balls. The second installation dominates Market Square at Oldmeldrum in Aberdeenshire. Created by Deeside artist Janet McEwan, a graduate of Aberdeen's Grays School of Art, the piece was financed in 2011 by the Scottish government's Town Centre Regeneration Fund, supported by Aberdeenshire Arts Development Team.

The artwork consists of three large granite spheres collectively called The Eternal Present: GNEISS GRANITE GABBRO. The design was inspired by several petrospheres unearthed at nearby Barra Hill and uses three varieties of local granite.

Alongside commissioning the sculpture, Aberdeenshire Council undertook extensive work intended to revitalise the town square, and a new and experimental 'courtesy traffic calming system' was put in place in the historic village centre. Based on the psychological principle that uncertainty is likely to reduce traffic speed, all of the junction markings and traffic signage on the main square were removed, forcing puzzled drivers to negotiate priorities at the various road junctions.

Oldmeldrum Market Square petrospheres sculpture. (© Duncan Harley)

Residents continue to have mixed feelings regarding this experimental traffic management scheme but are understandingly proud of the GNEISS GRANITE GABBRO sculpture.

ᔆᕽ ᔆᕽ ᔆᕽ

Port Elphinstone-born poet-sculptor James Pittendrigh Macgillivray must be one of Aberdeenshire's best-kept secrets. Born in 1856, Macgillivray trained in Glasgow under, among others, Banff-born sculptor William Brodie. Early on in his career Macgillivray produced exquisite busts of 'Glasgow Boy' painter Joseph Crawhall and philosopher Thomas Carlyle. His later works achieved international fame and include Edinburgh's Gladstone monument, the David Livingstone statue in Glasgow, the statue of Robert Burns in Irvine and the Lord Byron statue in Aberdeen.

Macgillivray was heavily influenced by Pictish designs and he is sometimes linked with the Scottish Renaissance movement of the 1920s. He is buried in Edinburgh's Gogar churchyard and his tombstone, which he himself carved in 1910 in memory of his wife Frieda, closely resembles the mysterious Pictish Maiden Stone that sits by the roadside at Pitcaple, near his home town of Inverurie.

Appointed King's Sculptor in Ordinary for Scotland in 1921, Macgillivray occasionally turned his hand to poetry and was also an accomplished musician. Amongst his verse is this oddity:

The Return (A Piper's Vaunting)
Och hey! for the splendour of tartans!
And hey for the dirk and the targe!
The race that was hard as the Spartans
Shall return again to the charge:
Shall come back again to the heather,
Like eagles, with beak and with claws
To take and to scatter for ever
The Sassenach thieves and their laws.
Och, then, for the bonnet and feather!
The pipe and its vaunting clear:
Och, then, for the glens and the heather!
And all that the Gael holds dear.

Many folk in the North-east are strongly of the opinion that Pittendrigh Macgillivray should have stuck with the sculpture!

ଚର ଚର ଚର

The Deeside town of Banchory sits in the lee of the Hill of Fare and enjoys a favourable climate in comparison to the towns further up the valley of the River Dee. However, a balmy day in summer is not the first thing to spring to mind when recalling the work of Deeside landscape artist Joseph Farquharson. Born in 1846 and heir to the family's Finzean estate, he is popularly associated with atmospheric paintings of sheep-littered winter landscapes. Affectionately known locally as 'The Painting Laird', Farquharson studied under French master Carolus-Duran, a contemporary of Édouard Manet. In the Paris of the 1880s, he became acquainted with the Barbizon school of painting. In warm summer weather, Barbizon artists ventured outdoors to paint directly from nature. Canvasses would typically be left on site, often for weeks at a time, until completed. On his return to Deeside, Joseph Farquharson adapted this *plein air*, or open air, technique for use at Northern latitudes. Having designed and built a series of mobile painting huts, complete with glazed panels and a wood stove, he would sit in reasonable comfort, painting Deeside landscapes in almost any weather, returning to part-completed work as and when favourable light and weather allowed.

It was his mastery of snowbound winter landscapes, often including flocks of sheep, which caught the public imagination. His 1883 Christmas card classic 'The

Joyless Winter Day', featuring a lonely shepherd tending his flocks in a raging Deeside blizzard, quickly became a bestseller. His sheep paintings presented many technical challenges, such as the fact that a flock of sheep cannot easily be persuaded to stand still. To solve this problem, Farquharson commissioned a flock of life-size plaster sheep from Monymusk-born craftsman William Wilson and used these to stake out the positions of the original live subjects in order to preserve the scene as the work progressed. It was apparently quite common at one time for folk in and around Banchory to stumble across his painting huts, complete with a dozen or so eerily silent and unmoving sheep, neatly arranged and awaiting the artist's return.

Best-selling Scottish artist Jack Vettriano was recently quoted as saying that whoever had rejected his paintings for the Royal Academy should 'Go and live in a cave'. Joseph Farquharson might well have agreed. Despite considerable financial success as an artist during his lifetime, and election to the Royal Academy in 1900, he was on occasion sneeringly referred to by some fellow artists as 'Frozen Mutton Farquharson'. Farquharson had the last laugh however when in 1985 Aberdeen Art Gallery hosted a retrospective of his work to mark the fiftieth anniversary of his death.

஘ ஘ ஘

The flight path into Aberdeen's Dyce Airport offers travellers spectacular aerial views of the Aberdeenshire landscape. Hills and lochs appear quite different when viewed from 10,000 ft or so and even well-known features can take on a completely new and unexpected form. One such landscape feature is Place of Origin in the village of Kemnay. Conceived as a piece of landscape art and officially opened by HRH the Duke of Kent in 2006, the sculpture addresses the long and important history of granite quarrying in Aberdeenshire. In its heyday, the quarry at Paradise Hill employed 400 men and much of the quarried stone went to make iconic structures such as Sydney Harbour Bridge and Marischal College in Aberdeen.

Ten years in the making, the Place of Origin artwork takes the form of a series of woodland walks and stone-built features culminating in a high vantage point where visitors can appreciate the sheer scale of the old quarry works within the surrounding landscape. The viewpoint is constructed using some 100,000 tons of quarry waste and draws inspiration from the various recumbent stone circles in the local landscape.

John Maine, one of the artists involved in the project, comments that:

> The underlying idea of Place of Origin was to lead people to a vantage point from which the Kemnay quarry would be revealed. In order to let viewers see the drama of the quarry without actually being exposed to the dangers of granite cliffs, we built a hill with a viewing platform high above the quarry workings.

Place of Origin sculpture at Kemnay. (© Duncan Harley)

The vantage point was created with the help of huge trucks and giant cranes: 'We would set out a circle of quarry blocks and then fill the middle with granite chippings. This final stage is therefore granite through and through.'

Among the tens of thousands of tons of quarry waste the artists involved in the project discovered a collection of jet black stones that were identified as having come all the way from India. Imported in order to provide an architectural highlight for the façades of otherwise grey granite buildings, these blocks now line the path leading to the top of the viewpoint, symbolically fulfilling their original function as a foil for the granite structure while also providing a welcome seat for the weary.

The artists involved suggest that Place of Origin shares an aesthetic sense with Japanese gardens in that it reflects the larger landscape it sits in. They were, however, startled when it became apparent that they had unwittingly created a landscape that, viewed from the air, took on a completely unexpected form. Images from above clearly show that the paths connecting the various elements of the vast sculpture closely resemble the sorts of patterns carved by Pictish sculptors on the various symbol stones found in the area. The artists had never planned to create a path network based on such imagery since it would, they felt, have seemed contrived.

Apparently the giant sculpture is visible to astronauts manning the International Space Station.

## ✢ ABERDEENSHIRE AVIATION ✢

Aberdeenshire is served by both an international airport and also a busy heliport serving North Sea oil exploration. In the twenty-first century the airport connects Aberdeen and Aberdeenshire to destinations around the globe and is Britain's fifth busiest airport in terms of total aircraft movement with around 3.76 million fixed-wing passengers passing through the airport each year; the heliport adds another 0.5 million helicopter passengers annually.

The airport was not always so busy. As North-east writer Mike Shepherd points out, its facilities in the very early days of the North Sea oil boom were at best woefully inadequate. 'Amazingly, in 1972,' writes Mike, 'the airport was quite basic and the arrivals and departures building was an old Nissen hut. One end was the

Captain Fresson's aircraft hangar at Cairnhall near Kintore. (© Duncan Harley)

bar and the other end was the tickets and seats. The same bloke did both jobs.' Facilities have fortunately improved in recent decades and the old Nissen hut was long ago replaced with a fit-for-purpose passenger terminal, but aviation in the north-east of Scotland has had a long and sometimes bizarre history.

Alongside the A96 at Cairnhall, on the outskirts of Kintore, there sits a fairly nondescript matt-black corrugated iron building of seemingly indeterminate age. Described by the Royal Commission on the Ancient and Historical Monuments of Scotland as 'Kintore Aircraft Hangar', the building has experienced several incarnations. In recent decades, it served as a water board store and is today occupied by an offshore equipment company. The category B-listed building was in fact erected in 1934 by air pioneer Captain Ernest Fresson, to house and service his airliners. Barnstormers such as Sir Alan Cobham's hugely popular Cobham's Flying Circus performed at Kintore in the 1930s but although Captain Fresson was not averse to providing occasional joyrides, his mission at Cairnhall was to develop the aerodrome for passenger and airmail operations.

Fresson first became interested in aviation in 1908. As a youngster, he had witnessed first-hand early flights by aviation pioneers such as Brabazon and Short. With a flying career that included Royal Flying Corps service on anti-U-boat patrols during the First World War, he quickly grasped the potential of commercial flying and, by 1934, was operating Britain's first airmail service to Orkney via Inverness. An Aberdeen–Orkney air route quickly followed, with flights taking off from a coastal grass airstrip at Seaton. The coming of the Royal Highland Show to Seaton, in 1935, meant that Fresson's airline, Highland Airways, would have to find an alternative local aerodrome. The airstrip at Dyce was unavailable, being at the time in the hands of a rival airline, and the captain began a desperate search for a replacement landing ground. In his memoirs, *The Air Road to the Isles*, he records the history of Kintore Airfield. The captain had recently purchased a 1920s DH.60 Gipsy Moth biplane from aviation pioneer Heloise 'Hailo' Pauer, and used the machine to scout out potential landing strips in the Aberdeenshire countryside. On arriving at Kintore, he approached a local farmer who, unable to spare the grazing land, recommended a neighbour who owned two fairly flat fields over by the cemetery. 'It was a good omen,' recalled Fresson in his autobiography, 'at least we would not have to look far in case of accident.'

Over a bottle of malt, the captain and the farmer at Cairnhall struck a deal. A hangar and an airstrip could be built on the site and a long lease was agreed. To sweeten the deal, the two men agreed that between flights, which averaged perhaps four per day, the farmer's dairy herd could continue to graze the landing ground.

Travel between Kintore Airfield and Orkney in those days cost £5.50 return and the airline flew in and out of Kintore using mainly DH.89A Dragon Rapides nine-seater, twin-engine biplanes. During the Second World War, the airstrips at Cairnhall and at neighbouring East Fingask at Oldmeldrum operated as dispersal aerodromes for RAF Dyce – nowadays better known as Aberdeen International Airport.

In his later years, Captain Fresson liked to entertain dinner guests with tales of the daring early days of Scottish aviation. One such story involved the search for a missing RAF Avro Anson aeroplane during spring 1941. While flying over the Cairngorms, Fresson claimed that he had not only located the 1941 crash site, but had also spotted the remains of a much older crash, dating from the winter of 1917. Seemingly, the 1917 wreck was that of a Royal Flying Corps Sopwith Camel that had gone missing without trace on a training flight out of Montrose Air Base. The captain's tale concludes with a vivid description of the tattered wreckage, wedged tightly in a snow-covered corrie, with the goggled and helmeted skeleton of the pilot still on board! First World War air historians have cast doubt on the authenticity of the captain's story, but whatever the truth of the matter, it does make for an interesting after dinner tale.

Bizarrely, even while Fresson was sharing the airfield at Kintore with grazing cattle, the farmer at Cairnhall was engaged in letting out the landing strip to an Inverurie businessman for horse racing. No wonder the captain chose the field beside the cemetery.

෨෨ ෨෨ ෨෨

In the 1930s public interest in aviation had never been higher and the phenomenon of the air circus had much to do with this. In 1933, Sir Alan Cobham's Flying Circus toured the North-east, performing at Kintore, Macduff and Huntly.

Friday, 14 July was show day. Despite rain, crowds filled the showground, a field on the outskirts of the market town of Huntly, to await the arrival of the flying circus. As the fourteen-strong air fleet swept in over the town, few present could have imagined the extent of the preparations made prior to the event. The complex nature of Cobham's Flying Circus required meticulous planning. The council, local landowners and local newspapers all had to be brought, and in some cases bought, onside. Permissions, suppliers and publicity had to be in place well before the event. To facilitate this, an advance crew visited the town, led by a manager whose job it was to arrange everything from hotel accommodation for the pilots to the selling of catering concessions to local companies. Crucially, the manager had to gain the cooperation of those landowners who could provide crop-free and level landing areas, often with the promise that they would make an absolute fortune after the show by selling off land for a 'proposed' Huntly International Airport. Local businesses were offered sponsorship deals and the Huntly Palace cinema ran a raffle for patrons, with a pleasure flight worth 5 shillings as the prize.

Provost Christie welcomed the fliers and, after a brief speech in which he enthused about the bright future of air travel, he encouraged the crowd to purchase

An early flying machine. (© Duncan Harley)

tickets for 'a flight, if not two'. He was treated to a complimentary joyride and then the show began in earnest.

Accompanied by a blaring commentary from the loudspeaker van, displays of 'Really Crazy Flying, Formation Aerobatics and Dancing in the Air' wowed the crowd. Wing walkers, a solo parachute descent and a scaled-down Schneider Cup Trophy Race followed. Aircraft flew through hoops, looped-the-loop and performed a manoeuvre mysteriously billed as 'Aerial Pig Sticking'. A highlight, described in the programme as a 'Surprise Item', involved a Cobham pilot disguised as a member of the crowd running on to the flying arena accompanied by shouts of 'Stop that man!' before taking off in a 'stolen' biplane. Once airborne, the thief performed several wobbly low-level circuits of the showground while waving excitedly to the crowd and making a great show of lighting his pipe mid-air. He then climbed out on to the wing, leaving the aircraft pilot-less. Unsurprisingly perhaps, a pilot was killed a year or so later performing this same stunt. After the evening performance, the Flying Circus moved on to the nearby coastal town of Macduff to repeat the entire performance next day.

Cobham was not the first to fly out of Huntly. The town's earliest brush with aviation came in 1910, when an advert in the *Huntly Express* announced that the famous aviator Douglas Gilmour was to take off from the town's Castle Park on 4 August. Apparently 2,000 people turned out to marvel at the spectacle. The owner of an early French-built Bleriot monoplane, Gilmour had a keen nose for publicity and was a favourite with the press, having gained national notoriety by bombing the Submarine Depot at Portsmouth with oranges, much to the embarrassment of the Navy.

The Huntly flight ended safely, the plane having landed in a field near the town's East Park Street, but Gilmour was killed two years later, in 1912, when his aircraft suffered structural failure over Richmond.

Another North-east aviation pioneer was George Davidson, born 1858. Known locally as 'Fleein Geordie', he is best remembered as the inventor of the steam-powered Davidson Air-Car. Davidson's designs tended to border on the bizarre. Weighing almost 8 tons, his Air-Car concept was ambitious to say the least. Nevertheless, between 1883 and 1897, he carried out local testing of early designs, culminating in a well-publicised flight attempt at Burnett Park in Banchory. In front of press and curious onlookers, Davidson took off in a scaled-down version of his monoplane, only to crash almost immediately. Unhurt apart from his bruised pride, he continued to develop his designs. An improved version of the Air-Car, renamed the 'Gyropter', was eventually manufactured in America, where Davidson's family had mining interests, but the project was finally abandoned following a catastrophic steam boiler explosion in 1906.

Fleein Geordie died at Inchmarlo Cottage, Banchory, in 1939 at the age of 80, having lived to see his predictions that aeroplanes would cross the Atlantic and be used to 'drop dynamite on our enemies' come true.

## ❖ BALNEOLOGY ❖

In the sixteenth and seventeenth centuries many wealthy landowners funded health spas on their estates and would invite the good and the great to 'take the waters' for medicinal and recreational purposes – a sort of hot tub experience, but without the heat perhaps.

Physicians began to set up shop beside the spas and would often recommend specific treatments such as cold baths, hot douches and, of course, the drinking of sea water. Textbooks such as *A Dissertation on the Use of Seawater in Diseases of the Glands*, published in 1750 by Dr Richard Russell, gave specific instructions on what nowadays might be regarded as legalised torture.

Scotland's national bard Robert Burns had strong links to the north-east of Scotland and on several occasions he toured the area, visiting relatives and gathering ballads for publication by Edinburgh music publisher James Johnson. He was in his later years a big fan of balneology.

Also known as 'medical bathing', balneology was popular in Burns's time and various proponents claimed that exposure to the effects of healing waters might affect a cure where all other treatments had failed. Dissertations were published and intense debate erupted among medical men as to the efficacy of cold spring water versus cold sea water in the curing of the sick.

Burns died on 21 July 1796 at just 37 and there are many theories as to the exact cause of his death. These range from venereal disease to rheumatic fever, with conditions such as liver cirrhosis and alcohol-induced seizure not far behind. The years of hard labour spent as a tenant farmer must also have taken their toll and exacerbated his already poor health. A more likely explanation is that the sickly bard died of fever after being advised by his doctor, William Maxwell, to bathe naked in freezing seawater. Robert Burns died within days of trying this curative treatment and was duly buried on 25 July 1796.

Logie Coldstone in Aberdeenshire is home to the lost wells of Poldhu. Hidden deep within the woods of Blelack and fed by natural spring water, the granite-lined mineral baths at Poldhu were once a popular attraction for those seeking cures for virtually any ailment. Mentioned in the First Statistical Account of Scotland (1791–99), they are described as 'a mineral spring in the parish [of Logie-

Poldhu Wells at Logie Coldstone. (© Duncan Harley)

Coldstone], a little to the S. of the church, called Poldow, which in Gaelic signifies "a black pool"; the water of which, some years ago, was much and successfully used for scorbutic and gravelish disorders'. By the time of the Second Statistical Account (1834–45), interest appears to have waned and the wells at Poldhu were said to be 'occasionally resorted to by some, for the benefit of their health, and by others for amusement'.

With time, a rhododendron thicket enveloped the wells and hid them from view. Recently, however, interest in the historic site was revived following the chance discovery of an old photograph showing the wells in use by members of the Cromar History Group. In 2008, with the help of various partnerships plus funding from the Adopt a Monument Fund, the accumulated vegetation surrounding the wells was removed, new drains were dug and the original stonework refurbished to the original Victorian design.

Nowadays, of course, there are no outlandish claims regarding cures for scorbutic or gravelish disorders.

∽ ∽ ∽

Ballater in Deeside is also home to a set of wells long known for their curative properties. The Pannanich Wells just outside the modern burgh first attracted national attention in 1760, when local Tullich woman Isabella Michie began bathing in the waters. She suffered from scrofula, or tuberculosis of the lymphatic glands. Scrofula was also known as the 'king's evil' and there was, at the time, a popular belief that the sovereign's touch could affect a cure. Indeed, monarchs including Edward the Confessor and Louis XV of France reportedly 'touched' hundreds of victims at a time during grand ceremonies designed to show that the sovereign's right to rule was God-given and that divine intervention came via the royal palms. There is little likelihood that Isabella had actually been touched by royalty so her complete recovery, from what was an often-fatal disease, was put down to the curative properties of the Pannanich Wells. Word spread like wildfire. However, the Ballater of 1760 was not quite ready to cope with the influx of visitors. In fact, it largely consisted of bleak empty moorland with few dwellings or creature comforts for the visitor. The railways were not to arrive until 1866 and the road system was quite primitive, lacking even a bridge over the River Dee.

Pannanich Wells at Ballater. (© Duncan Harley)

Now, Deeside landowner Francis Farquharson of Monaltrie had fought on the losing side at Culloden and was consequently taken to London's New Gaol at Southwark in an overcrowded prison ship where, alongside the majority of Jacobite officers, he was condemned to be hung. On the night of 27 November 1746, shortly before his scheduled execution, Farquharson was reprieved following the granting of a petition for clemency. Exiled for twenty years, he returned to Ballater in 1766 and immediately began improvements designed to provide employment and prosperity for the area. Impressed by Isabella Michie's miracle cure, he built the granite facings that to this day grace the well heads at the upper and lower Pannanich Wells and he then set about the construction of lodgings and bath houses to accommodate the new health tourism industry.

As the wells grew in popularity, so Ballater grew in stature. Some locals even took to verse. Reverend Dr John Ogilvie, minister at nearby Midmar, penned the following lines in 1795:

I've seen the sick to health return
I've seen the sad forget to mourn
I've seen the lame their crutches burn
And loup and fling at Pannanich
I've seen the auld seem young and frisky
Without the aid of ale or whisky
I've seen the dullest hearts grow brisky
At blithesome, helpful Pannanich.

Nowadays water from Pannanich is exported worldwide by the Deeside Water Company. Owner Martin Simpson includes Japan, Switzerland and even the Kremlin on his export list and tells visitors: 'When you consider that there was virtually nothing here up until 1760, the springs with their proven health-giving properties made Ballater what it is today.'

Queen Victoria undoubtedly would have heard about Pannanich since her summer residence at Balmoral was just a few miles away. When her consort, the Prince Albert, approached 40 his health went into a serious decline and Victoria told friends that he seemed 'somewhat of a hypochondriac', commenting that 'as usual, desponding as men really are when unwell … he is not inclined himself to admit that he is better.'

In December 1861, the poor man died at Windsor of what may have been typhoid fever and the figurehead of the British Empire entered into what has often been described as a deep and melancholic depression. Perhaps if Albert had taken the time to drink from the Pannanich Wells, the course of British history might have been completely different.

## ❧ THE BEATLES ❧

Mention The Beatles in the context of Aberdeenshire and most folk will recall the Fab Four's 1963 Scottish tour. The tour began on 3 January and included performances in Elgin, Dingwall and Bridge of Allan. The final gig took place on Sunday, 6 January at Aberdeen Beach Ballroom, where the group were apparently booed while on stage following a reported 'mixed reaction' from the assembled crowd.

John Lennon, Paul McCartney, George Harrison and Ringo Starr had been billed as a supporting act for Johnny Scott and his Big Band and the group's set, consisting mainly of Buddy Holly and Ricky Nelson covers, seemingly suffered from a less than perfect sound system. After being paid a mere £45 for the Beach Ballroom gig, The Beatles went on to play to audiences around the globe. They never returned to Aberdeen, but did play in Madison Square Gardens and Tokyo's Nippon Budokan, as well as in a few hundred other international stadiums. However, it almost never happened. Three years earlier, in May of 1960, Johnny Gentle, a pop idol from the same stable as Billy Fury and Marty Wilde, was dispatched by his manager to tour the dance halls of the North-east. Backing him were some youngsters from Liverpool calling themselves The Silver Beetles. In those early days, the group toured in a battered old Austin 16 van, staying in budget hotels along the way. They were paid £60, plus travel expenses,

The Beatles first toured in Aberdeenshire during May 1960. (Courtesy of Janice Rayne)

for the entire tour and, until an hour before the first performance, they had never even met Johnny Gentle.

London-based promoter Larry Parnes had hired an elderly Scottish pig farmer by the name of Duncan McKinnon as tour manager and, following an unscheduled stop for some rest and recreation, the road trip nearly ended in tragedy. The first gig was at Alloa on 20 May and the set comprised cover versions of popular hits including Buddy Holly's 'It Doesn't Matter Anymore', 'I Need Your Love Tonight' by Elvis Presley, and 'He'll Have to Go' by Jim Reeves. In short, there wasn't a Lennon and McCartney piece within hearing range. The same set was to be repeated slavishly throughout the tour. What's more, George was billed as 'Carl Harrison', John as 'Johnny Lennon' and Paul went by the pseudonym of 'Paul Ramone'. In the publicity material 'The Silver Beetles' name was largely unused, the band being billed as 'Johnny Gentle and his Group'.

After Alloa, the young hopefuls performed at Fraserburgh, Keith, Forres and Nairn, with a final gig at Peterhead's Rescue Hall. In all, they are said to have driven more than 700 miles in the overloaded Austin van. This gruelling travel schedule, not to mention the late nights and early starts, nearly led to disaster – and a small autograph book owned by a young lass from Banff holds the key to what happened.

Plaque commemorating the Silver Beetles' 1960 tour. (© Duncan Harley)

In September 2004, Christie's advertised 'Lot 204/Sale 9919', comprising:

A very rare, early set of autographs, 23 May, 1960, on five pages from an autograph book signed and inscribed during the Beatles' first ever tour of Scotland, one page signed in blue ballpoint pen by Paul McCartney and George Harrison with their then stage names Paul Ramon and Carl Harrison and by John Lennon as Johnny Lennon, the page additionally inscribed in McCartney's hand The Beatles, another page signed and inscribed in blue ballpoint pen love Stuart xx [Sutcliffe], additional pages signed and inscribed Thomas Moore, Drums; love Johnny Gentle; and With best wishes, Margie xx.

The item fetched £5,019 at auction.

The Silver Beetles' tour van, Johnny Gentle at the wheel, had crashed into a saloon car outside the autograph book owner's house, near Banff, whilst heading to Fraserburgh. According to one account, the band's regular driver, Gerry Scott, had wanted a rest from driving and Johnny Gentle, a sleeping Lennon by his side – both perhaps a little the worse for wear in those pre-breathalyser days – had driven straight into the rear of a Ford Popular saloon car at a crossroads on the A98.

The journey had been punctuated by a stop-over at an Aberdeenshire pig farm involving consumption of copious amounts of bacon and eggs, washed down with similarly copious amounts of Mackeson Stout. The occupants of the saloon car were reportedly 'all shook up', but otherwise unharmed. The elderly husband and wife had been on a shopping trip to Aberdeen and, of course, could have had no idea at the time how close the accident had been to completely changing the course of British pop music. Tour drummer Tommy Moore was not so lucky. The impact had sent a flying guitar directly into his face and he was taken by ambulance to the local cottage hospital, suffering broken teeth and cuts.

According to the Christie's sale brochure, in the aftermath of the road accident John Lennon had asked the young autograph book owner where the nearest fish and chip shop was, before deciding to wait at the scene until the police arrived. The young pop fan then went off to buy chips for the musicians and, on her return, Lennon told her to keep the change while the entire band signed her autograph book. The 'Margie' who signed 'With best wishes, Margie xx' was seemingly Marjorie Overall, Johnny Gentle's girlfriend at the time, whose striking peroxide-mauve hair and tight mauve trousers must have stood out like a beacon in 1960s rural Aberdeenshire.

Following the accident, the dented but still serviceable van continued on to Fraserburgh, arriving in the seaside fisher town at about 3 p.m. in plenty of time for the evening performance, but of course minus one drummer. The Silver Beetles would probably have managed to perform without a drummer, but the local organiser of the gig insisted that since he'd paid for a drummer, a drummer was what he wanted. So the luckless, and by now semi-sedated, Tommy Moore was literally dragged from his hospital bed by his band and transported to the venue, where he was grumpily seated behind his drums and strongly encouraged to perform. His painful if not life-threatening injuries, and his growing disillusionment with a life on the road, led him to wonder if his past employment in a Liverpool milk bottle factory might be preferable to a life on the road with a pop group.

After further gigs including Peterhead, The Silver Beetles changed their name to The Beatles, referencing the 'beat' generation and Jack Kerouac's *On the Road*. 'Paul Ramone' became Paul McCartney, 'Johnny Lennon' reverted to John Lennon, and 'Carl Harrison' became George Harrison. The rest is history and, decades on, the contribution to the music scene of the first real mega-group is still being felt. Mind you, given that potentially serious accident on the road to Fraserburgh in May 1960, it very nearly never happened.

## ☙ CASTLES ❧

Known as 'castle country', Aberdeenshire is home to over 150 castles. Some, such as Drum, Crathes and Fyvie castles, are in the care of the National Trust for Scotland and have been lovingly preserved. Many more are in ruins and awaiting the kind hand of the restorer.

Delgatie Castle at Turriff is a splendid example of a restored castle and dates from about AD 1030. Now run by a private trust, the castle was owned by the Hay family for a large part of the last 650 years, having been taken from Henry de Beaumont, Earl of Buchan, following Robert the Bruce's rout of the English army at the Battle of Bannockburn. The earl had unwisely taken the English side and, after accompanying Edward II in his flight from the field, he became one of many nobles affected by a sentence of forfeiture passed by the Scottish Parliament.

The most recent Hay to occupy the castle was Captain 'Jock' Hay of Delgatie, who took over the running of the property in the 1950s following a long military career. After soldiering in India where, prior to Partition, he commanded a fort near the Afghan border, he had returned to Scotland to plan Home Guard preparations for a feared German invasion of Shetland. When hostilities came to an end, he took over management of the family's Shetland estate before, with his wife Everild, embarking on a quite remarkable restoration project at Delgatie. Literally decades of hard work have resulted in the Delgatie Castle visitor experience of today. A popular attraction is 'Queen Mary's Bower', a small room high in the tower where Mary Queen of Scots stayed for several days following the Battle of Corrichie in 1562.

Delgatie Castle trustee Joan Johnson has fond memories of the captain. Describing him as a towering 6ft 7in eccentric in feathered bonnet and kilt, she says: 'You couldn't miss him; we often opened the newspaper or turned on the news to find that he was being featured attending some SNP conference or other. The press seemed to love him.'

Joan recalls: 'When he bought Delgatie, it was in a very run-down state.' Owned at the time by the Countess of Errol, it had been a field hospital in the Second World War and was in danger of having its roof removed to reduce taxation. Joan continues:

Delgatie Castle near Turriff. (© Duncan Harley)

> The Captain was determined to buy and restore the castle, so he took out his cheque book and wrote the countess a cheque for every penny he owned. He then returned home to his wife to tell her that he loved her very much and had, in consequence, bought her a castle!

Further south at Stonehaven lies the stunning cliff top ruins of Dunnottar Castle. The fortification is one of the outstanding ancient monuments of Scotland and stands high up on a precipitous outcrop of rock jutting out into the North Sea. To reach the castle, visitors face a challenging walk along a gravel path from the car park, then down 178 steps, along another path, then up another ninety steps to the main gate.

Beside featuring as a twenty-first-century screensaver on Microsoft Windows 7, the castle is well-remembered as the defender and saviour of the Scottish crown jewels. The regalia – a crown, sceptre and sword – had been placed within the fortress walls prior to Cromwell's eight-month siege in 1651. Some time during the siege, no one is quite certain when, the royal regalia were smuggled out to be hidden at nearby Kinneff church, leaving the besieging army with a somewhat hollow victory.

Dunnottar has been besieged many times, both by foreign invaders such as the Vikings and by the home-grown armies of Cromwell, James Graham, 1st Marquis of Montrose plus, of course, William Wallace. Cromwell and Montrose seem to have contented themselves with burning nearby Stonehaven while Wallace infamously burned the castle's church in 1297, with the English garrison imprisoned inside. 'Blind Harry', the Scots *makar* or bard, recounts the event in his epic poem *Wallace*:

> Therefore a fire was brought speedily,
> Which burnt the church, and all those South'ron boys,
> Out o'er the rock the rest rush'd great noise;
> Some hung on craigs, and loath were to die,
> Some lap, some fell, some flutter'd in the sea,
> And perish'd all, not one remain'd alive.

In a move lauded by some, the Dunnottar ruin have been included in a recent smartphone app allowing tourists around the globe to experience a virtual tour of Dunnottar without actually visiting the place. Despite this new initiative the keepers of the castle claim that around 100,000 folk visit the site each year.

Mary Queen of Scots famously slept at Dunnottar not once but twice. Her first overnight was on her journey south after the Battle of Corrichie in 1562 and she returned in 1564 during the course of a 'Perambulation' – a sort of sixteenth-century equivalent of Prime Minister's Question Time.

Magnificent even in decay, and in the care of Historic Scotland, Huntly Castle occupies the site of a much earlier fortified building. The 1st Marquis of Huntly completed the structure in around 1606 and over the years it has sheltered, among others, Robert the Bruce and Mary of Guise, the mother of Mary Queen of Scots. Unusually, perhaps, there appears to be no claim that Mary herself slept within its walls, although the building was pillaged on her orders in 1562. Famed for possessing the most unpleasant dungeon in the whole of Scotland, the building became a garrison for government troops during the 1745 Jacobite Rebellion since Huntly, like many Scottish towns, was a hotbed of Jacobite sentiment.

Confusingly, Huntly Castle is also known in some circles as Strathbogie Castle and sits within the boundaries of the town of Milton of Strathbogie, nowadays better known as Huntly. The unwary sometimes confuse the fortification with HM Castle Huntly, a fifteenth-century castle near Dundee, which is currently used as an open prison.

The commuter town of Kintore at one time boasted two castles. Hallforest Castle, today a ruin, stands a mile west of the town. Visited by Mary Queen of Scots in 1562, the 60ft tower house is visible from the A96 and is a rare example of a fourteenth-century Scottish keep. What remained of a second fortress, on the Castle Hill, in the centre of the town, fell victim to the Victorian obsession with rail travel.

A conical mound over 30ft high, this second fortress was compared to the historic Bass, at nearby Inverurie. Sadly, the twelfth-century monument lay directly

Hallforest Castle near Kintore.
(© Duncan Harley)

in the path of the Great North of Scotland Railway and was completely flattened around 1854 to make way for the Aberdeen–Inverness line. No visible traces remain above ground and even the exact location is now uncertain.

Visible from all points of the compass, the 30ft-high ruined medieval castle on the summit of the 879ft-high Dunnideer Hill dominates the landscape around Insch. Ranked in historical importance alongside the nearby hill forts of Tap O' Noth and Mither Tap, Dunnideer hill fort sits among much older structures. Site records from Historic Environment Scotland indicate that although the castle is traditionally thought to have been erected by Gregory the Great in AD 890, it was more likely constructed by David, Earl of Huntingdon and Garioch, in 1178, largely using materials from an earlier vitrified fort. It may represent the earliest authenticated example of a tower house in Scotland. Around the structure there are clearly defined turf ramparts and obvious remains of mysterious vitrified fortifications.

There is a centuries-old tradition that the teeth of sheep grazed on the hill of Dunnideer turn to gold because there is gold ore hidden deep underground. Some sources point to iron pyrites as being the likely source of the legend. Others assert that the golden discoloration is down to dental encrustation caused by a chemical reaction between ovine saliva, lime and phosphoric oxide.

Seemingly the phenomenon is not confined to the sheep of Dunnideer since many other mammals worldwide, including camels, hippopotami and even Cretan goats, have exhibited similar symptoms. Locals dismiss the iron pyrites theory and darkly hint that there are long-lost mine workings on the north face of the hill. Be that as it may, the ground around the castle has yielded several ancient artefacts, including a *gladius* or short sword possibly left behind by a Roman soldier some 2,000 years ago.

The Bass motte and bailey castle at Inverurie, locally known simply as 'the Bass', consists of two flat-topped conical hillocks, the largest of which stands a full 39ft above the surrounding graveyard. Such castles were once common throughout Scotland, although many have been overlaid by later stone-built fortifications. Although nowadays it is recognised as a naturally occurring geological feature, legends and fantastical theories abound regarding the origins of the Bass: a burial mound containing the remains of plague victims, a place of hidden buried treasure or a fire signal station dating from the times of the Danish invaders are just a few suggestions.

In June 1944, on the very eve of D-Day, the Bass was subjected to intensive study by a paranormal investigator who concluded that the site was the dwelling place of a group of monstrous spirits, buried by druids so as to frustrate the 'Evil Earth Magnetism of the Mound of Death!'

Dunnideer Hill Fort. (© Duncan Harley)

The Bass of Inverurie. (© Duncan Harley)

The investigator was John Foster Forbes. Forbes can really only be described as an eccentric. Born at Rothiemay in Aberdeenshire in 1889, he served in the First World War as intelligence officer before embarking on a career as a teacher. He had a fascination for prehistory and took to investigating the many Neolithic and Pictish monuments of his home county. His investigation of the Bass at Inverurie was carried out in the company of a psychic by the name of Iris Campbell who *tuned into* the mound using a procedure known as psychometry. Seemingly the two investigators were completely traumatised by what they discovered at the site and it took them several days to shake off the malign influence of the 'Mound of Death'.

Whatever the truth of the matter, the Bass probably once hosted the administrative centre of the earldom of the Garioch during the twelfth century. Nowadays, it presides over the residents of the town's old cemetery.

## ⁑ CATTLE ⁑

Agricultural development in Aberdeenshire owes much to the improvements in communication and transport brought about both by the Aberdeenshire Canal in the early nineteenth century and the arrival of the railways from around 1850. For the first time, key agricultural inputs such as guano and the euphemistically named 'night soil' or inner-city dung collected from neighbouring cities and towns could be ploughed into the land. Exports such as slate, wheat and oats could be sold both abroad and across the UK, providing revenue to sustain further development; the economy of the county was soon booming.

Alongside the vastly improved crop yields, there was a movement amongst the agricultural community to improve livestock breeds. One of the most famous of these, the Aberdeen Angus, was to achieve international fame largely through the ingenuity of William McCombie, a farmer and stock breeder from Tillyfourie near Alford.

Nowadays, of course, there is strong demand for the breed and prices often top 18,000 guineas for bulls with good breeding potential. In Victorian times, prices were more uncertain but, thanks mainly to the breeder from Alford, the Aberdeen Angus breed was destined for stardom both on and off the dinner table.

On 12 June 1878, a ponderously titled farming journal, *The North British Agriculturist*, published an article honouring McCombie, Scotland's 'Cattle King'. The previous Sunday, McCombie had carried off top honours for livestock at the Paris Exposition Universelle, better known perhaps as the Third Paris World Fair. 'This is indeed a proud week for Tillyfour and for the polled Angus or Aberdeen breed of cattle ... Mr McCombie having been adjudged the £100 prize for the best group of cattle, bred by exhibitor and reared out of France,' ran the article: 'McCombie's successful group numbered six animals ... every black polled animal has a ticket of some kind!'

Preparations for the Paris Exposition had involved major upgrading of the French railway network, and it is fair to assume that McCombie's cows had travelled in some comfort from Alford to Paris by train, before alighting at the delightfully named Gare du Champ de Mars, alongside the Eiffel Tower.

The Alford farmer was in good company. The likes of Thomas Edison and Alexander Graham Bell were in attendance and the very latest industrial designs filled the giant exhibition halls. Steam ploughs and ice-making machines vied with monoplanes and electric arc lamps for the attention of the 13 million visitors. Indeed, with the notable exception of Germany, which had until 1871 been at war with France, the industrialised countries of the world descended on the French capital to showcase the very best in international design.

Alongside the industrial halls, the 66-acre site featured show rings for the judging of premium European livestock. In all, 1,700 cattle, 825 sheep and 380 pigs were entered for the various competitions. McCombie was, by then, quite used to exhibition success, with a track record of wins occupying seventeen pages in the 1875 edition of his breed book, *Cattle and Cattle Breeders*. Gold medals, winners' cups and cash prizes came his way by the dozen, and by the time of his death, in 1880, he was recognised as the 'great deliverer of the polled race', a reference to the fact that pure-bred Aberdeen Angus are devoid of horns.

McCombie's success in the show ring was down to both careful management of his breeding programme and a quite brilliant flair for publicity. His Tillyfourie-

Janice Rayne and Aberdeen Angus Sculpture at Alford. (© Duncan Harley)

bred bull Black Prince, for example, was invited to a royal audience with Queen Victoria at Windsor Royal Farm, in recognition of his successive wins at Smithfield and Birmingham Fat Stock Shows. When the animal was finally 'retired', around 1867, McCombie presented the monarch with a 90kg baron of beef, sufficient to feed sixty people, from the carcass.

A year or so later, when the Queen travelled to Alford from Balmoral to inspect the Tillyfourie herd, she was surprised to meet Black Prince once again. McCombie had kept the animal's head, which now hung, stuffed, in a prominent position on the wall of his dining room.

The Aberdeen Angus breed has its origins long before William McCombie. Indeed, the herd book, or bible of the breed, records Hugh Watson's bull Old Jock, from Keillor of Newtyle in Angus, as the originator of the bloodline we see today. McCombie is, however, widely regarded as the great improver of the breed and a life-size statue of his legacy stands on the southern approach to Alford, in the form of 'Jeremy-Eric', a Kemnay-bred prize-winning bull from the 1990s. Unveiled by the Prince of Wales and the late Queen Mother, in perhaps her last Scottish public engagement, artist David Annand's bronze statue is a fitting reminder of the role played by William McCombie in making the town of Alford famous, as the home of the Aberdeen Angus.

ᕙᕗ ᕙᕗ ᕙᕗ

Located on the very edge of the Cairngorm National Park, and with the 25,000-acre Glen Tanar estate literally on the doorstep, the Deeside town of Aboyne is steeped in centuries of rich history and offers visitors a unique Royal Deeside experience. Alongside the traditional hunting, shooting and fishing, the town boasts a shooting range built inside a former Royal Deeside railway tunnel, a fine castle and an annual Highland Games. The town is also home to the 'Coos Cathedral'.

Due largely to the efforts of Sir William Cunliffe-Brooks, an eccentric Victorian banker and MP for East Cheshire, Glen Tanar – Tana – as Sir William preferred to call his estate, features architecture more usually seen in the likes of Kent than in Highland Aberdeenshire. Deeside architect Mike Rassmussen once described the man as a keen amateur architect who had a hand in designing all the cottages, farms and school buildings on the estate, as well as Glen Tanar House. Sir William, a keen country sportsman, liked nothing better than to treat his many wealthy and important guests to what might be considered a nineteenth-century version of the Highland Tinchal, or Great Hunt. To this end he commissioned estate kennels, complete with electric light and central heating, for his fifty or so hunting dogs. In 1887, in a fit of supreme extravagance, he built the spectacular Tower of Ess, at the Glen Tanar estate entrance, in a clear bid to impress visitors. But perhaps his most eccentric undertaking was the construction of a grand cowshed, fit for that noblest of beasts, the Aberdeen Angus.

The Coos Cathedral at Aboyne. (© Duncan Harley)

Completed in 1889, at a cost of £6,000, the Coos Cathedral was designed to accommodate around forty cows and several pedigree bulls in grey granite luxury. Complete with granary, turnip store and workers' accommodation, the massive steading, with its high-beamed ceilings, even featured a miniature tramway for the carrying in of feed and, of course, the transporting out of dung. Following decades of neglect, the building, set within the grounds of the historic Aboyne Castle, has found a new use as a venue for wedding receptions and corporate events. The Coos have, of course, been evicted in favour of paying guests.

∞ ∞ ∞

The Aberdeenshire town of Turriff is invariably associated with the 'Turra Coo' episode. Lloyd George's 1909 'People's Budget' had far-reaching effects throughout the UK. The bill proposed welfare reforms, to be funded by National Insurance contributions, and included land valuation taxes aimed at the rich. The proposed legislation led to a constitutional stand-off when the House of Lords vetoed the proposals, perhaps fearing the thin end of the socialist wedge. Following much debate in Parliament, including statements by the Welsh-born chancellor, such as: 'A fully-equipped duke costs as much to keep as two dreadnought battleships,' but 'is much less easy to scrap', the Parliament Act of 1911 deprived the Lords of their power of veto.

When the National Health Insurance Act of 1911 came into force as a consequence of the 1909 budget, folk in Turriff, and indeed in many towns throughout Scotland, were incensed at what they perceived as state interference in local affairs. Meetings were held during which hecklers shouted down speakers sent to persuade them of the benefits of health insurance. Effigies of Lloyd George were burned in the square at Inverurie and, in Turriff, feelings ran high among both farm workers and their employers.

What happened next is still remembered in the town. Popular local farmer Robert Paterson, of Lendrum, became the focus of sheriff officers when he refused to pay the National Insurance contributions due for his workforce. As a consequence, one of his milk cows was seized, to be sold at auction to pay the debt. After some often hilarious and widely reported events, including the pelting of the local bobbies with eggs and the painting of slogans such as 'Frae Lendrum to Leeks' on the poor cow's flanks, in reference to the chancellor's Welsh heritage, the animal was eventually returned to Lendrum Farm to live out the rest of her days blissfully unaware of her celebrity status.

A full-size bronze statue of the animal now stands at 'Coo Corner', on Turriff's High Street, and a few miles south, at Lendrum Farm, there is a memorial plaque commemorating those events of over a century ago.

The Turra Coo memorial at Lendrum. (© Duncan Harley)

Aberdeenshire poet Bob Smith penned a poem in the local Doric dialect entitled 'Braw Image o' the Coo' describing the entire episode:

A bronze statue o the Turra Coo
Noo staans proodly in the toon
Ti commemorate a gweed story
A've kent since a wis a loon
The fite coo fae Lendrum
Wis the celebrity o it's day
Fin fairmer Robert Paterson
Thocht NI wisna fair play
Sheriff Geordie Keith set oot
Tae seize property as a fine
Bit the locals widna help him
An refused tae tae the line
The coo wis pit up fer auction
Fegs iss nearly caused a riot

Syne up steps Alexander Craig
As the bodie faa wid buy it
Noo iss is nae the eyn o the story
Fowk an injustice they hid seen
A fair pucklie did rally roon
Wi fairmer Craig a deal wis deen
The coo wis noo back at Lendrum
Tae see oot the rest o her days
Nae doot neen the wiser o
The stooshie she did raise
At a junction in the bonnie toon
Iss a sculture o the beast
Faa brocht a fair bit o fame
Tae Turra an the haill north-east.

While many towns in Aberdeenshire choose to simply repaint local post boxes in honour of their prize-winning athletes and Olympians, Inverurie folk have taken the trouble to repaint a local cow to celebrate a Commonwealth gold.

Folk tales about the market town of Inverurie range from the 'Hound and Hare' mark on the bridge over the River Ury to the story of the Golden Cow. The tale of the Hound and Hare features a hare hunt in some forgotten year or other and involves a pack of the laird's foxhounds pursuing a solitary hare over the bridge over the Ury, at the Bass. Depending on which version you adhere to, the hare either escapes by leaping from the parapet into the waters below, or suffers blunt

Inverurie's Golden Cow. (© Duncan Harley)

force trauma on the sharp rocks below the bridge, closely followed by the pack of suicidal canines. The bridge's parapet helpfully bears the faintly incised capital letter 'H' to mark the spot where the infamous leap allegedly took place.

Inverurie's Golden Cow tale is more concise and involves a fibreglass ruminant that, each day at dawn, is wheeled on to the pavement outside Mitchell's Dairy and each evening is wheeled back inside, perhaps in a move to avoid rustlers.

Originally a Friesian, the animal was recently repainted in gold, in honour of Inverurie athlete Hannah Miley's gold medal win at the 2014 Glasgow Commonwealth Games, in the 400m individual swimming medley.

## ✤ CORNKISTERS ✤

Bothys are outbuildings on farms in Scotland where unmarried farm labourers lived, often in harsh conditions. In the evenings, to entertain themselves they used to sing songs, often termed 'bothy ballads'. Inevitably, many humorous airs arose critical of working conditions on farms. The term 'cornkister' refers to a song or the singer of a song, generally comic, voiced in Doric and written in the tradition of the 'bothy ballads'. The name refers to the *kist*, or chest, used to store oats for the farm horses. The singer typically sat on top of the cornkist and kicked their heels against it in time to the music.

A typical Aberdeenshire bothy. (© Duncan Harley)

One of the best-known cornkisters is 'The Barnyards o Delgaty':

As ah gaed doon tae Turra Merket,
Turra Merket fur tae fee,
Ah met in wi a wealthy fairmer,
He promised me the twa best horse
I ever set my een upon.
When ah gaed hame tae the Barnyards
There was nothin there but skin and bone.
The auld grey mare sat on her hunkers,
The auld dun horse lay in the grime.
For aa that I would 'hup' and cry,
They wouldna rise at yokin time.
When I gang tae the kirk on Sunday,
Mony's the bonny lass I see,
Sittin by her faither's side,
Winkin ower the pews at me.
Some can drink and no be drunk,
And some can fecht and no be slain.
I can coort anither man's lass,
And aye be welcome tae my ain.
Ma candle noo is fair brunt oot,
The snotter's fairly on the wane,
Fare ye weel, ye Barnyards,
Ye'll never catch me here again!

The young ploughman at Delgaty had gone to the market town of Turriff to 'fee' or to gain a period of employment on a farm. The farmer had engaged him on the promise of two fine plough horses, but of course, he had lied through his teeth!

The market town of Oldmeldrum has a strong association with Cornkisters. Morris's Hotel is probably the oldest building in town and the gable end of Jock's Bar, at the 1673 former coffee house, sports plaques commemorating previous residents, including 'King o' the Cornkisters' Willie Kemp (1889–1965) and George Morris, writer of many popular comic songs. Willie was signed up to the Beltona record label and made frequent radio broadcasts from the BBC's Aberdeen studios in the 1920s. His output included classics such as 'Willie Gillander's Goat' and 'The Weddin' o' McGinnis to his Cross-Eyed Pet'. Known as 'The Buchan Chiel', George Morris (1876–1958) married Willie's sister, Agnes, in 1912 and moved to Oldmeldrum, where he, too, signed with Beltona. His output included 'The Buchan Bobby', 'Aikey Brae' and 'A New Lum Hat'. Perhaps his best-known composition, still widely sung today, is 'A Pair o Nicky Tams', which includes the immortal lines:

Though unco sweir, I took them aff, the lassie for the please,
But aye my breeks they lirkit up, a roon aboot my knees.
A wasp gaed crawlin up my leg, in the middle o the Psalms,
So niver again will I rig the kirk withoot my Nicky Tams.

Nicky Tams were bindings tied tightly below the trouser-knee to stop mud and wee beasties getting to where they shouldn't get to. Known as *taums*, they made the wearer's breeks resemble knickerbockers.

Traditional singer Jimmy MacBeath was born in Portsoy in 1894, and is buried in the town. Jimmy was an itinerant worker and a singer well known for his warm and husky voice. A Gordon Highlander during the First World War, he hailed from travelling folk and was prone to tramp the highways and byways earning money along the way by singing at markets and in pubs. Between the wars he found work in the logging camps of Canada but despite all the hard work, the soldiering and the singing, he never became a wealthy man. Like many before him, he liked good company and a good drink.

In a *Scotsman* article penned by Jim Gilchrist long after Jimmy's death, Portsoy Folk Club Chairman Bob Philips recalls his first encounter with the man at Aberdeen Grammar School: 'Jimmy's not so covert libations from a half bottle concealed in a brown paper bag almost got the school folk club closed down by the affronted authorities.'

In 1951, he had his big break when he signed with Columbia Records and carved out a professional career, performing the likes of 'The Barnyards of Delgaty' and 'Fae Would Be a Fisherman's Wife' in early black-and-white folk programmes on the BBC. One of his recorded stories, 'Bonny Portsoy, You're Aa Ma Ain', leaves no doubt about his feelings for his home town. He died in 1972 in an Aberdeen hospital.

After Jimmy passed, the singer and folk song collector Hamish Henderson commented that :'Money always flowed through Jimmy's hands like water. He spent quite a lot on booze and was always ready to stand his hand in company.' Jimmy was for a time buried in an unmarked grave in Portsoy Parish Kirkyard but in 1999 local folk, mindful of his contribution to Portsoy's heritage, erected a headstone bearing the inscription 'Bound to be a row' in reference to the likelihood of Jimmy creating a major ruction in the hereafter.

To this day, members of the local folk club gather in June each year, on the anniversary of his death, to sing loudly around Jimmy's grave.

### ❖ DEVILISHNESS ❖

Approximately 20 per cent of all Pictish stones recorded in Scotland can be found in Aberdeenshire. The Maiden Stone at Drumdurno, just a few miles north of Inverurie, is perhaps the finest free-standing example of these ancient monoliths in the whole of Europe and despite the stone's, obvious Pictish heritage, local folklore hints that it is in fact the work of the devil.

Making a pact with the devil is rarely a good idea. But that is exactly what the Maiden of Drumdurno did, albeit unwittingly, many years ago. The daughter of a local farmer, she was apparently the *belle* of the parish and, in consequence, had accumulated a number of suitors. Ultimately, only one was fortunate enough to gain a promise of marriage and the unsuccessful candidates quietly retired to lick their wounds before setting out to woo another.

With one single exception, they wished her a long and happy life with her chosen one. The odd man out harboured thoughts of vengeance. One dark night as he wandered around the dark woods of the Pittodrie estate, he planned revenge on his rival. No sooner had he uttered the words: 'Oh that my eternal destruction could plague their earthy peace, how soon and sure the bargain would be mine' than Beelzebub himself appeared saying, 'Capital wish! I'll do the thing for you on your own terms.' A bargain was quickly concluded and the two made off on their separate ways.

On the day before the wedding, the maiden was busy baking bannocks for the wedding feast. As she baked, a handsome stranger entered the kitchen. 'It sets ye weel to bake lass,' he began. 'Gin ye had only mair speed at it!' She replied, 'I dinna' ken whether it sets me weel or no … but I think few could grudge my speed.' After some further light banter, the stranger suggested a competition. He wagered that he could lay a causeway to the very top of the nearby hill of Bennachie before she could finish her baking; if he won the bet, her hand and her heart should be his. Deeming the proposal just a harmless piece of fun, the lassie agreed, whereupon the stranger went off on his way and the maiden resumed the task in hand.

By evening, with the bannocks almost baked, she had quite forgotten the encounter and was thinking only of her impending wedding. The night was gloomy and wet and as she looked out the window for the arrival of her betrothed, the clouds parted and a full moon lit up the hill of Bennachie. There, shining brightly in the moonlight was a brand-new path running all the way from her very door to the hilltop. At that moment the kitchen door flew open and the stranger, whom she now realised was the Prince of Darkness, entered to claim her as his prize.

In panic and realising her mistake, the poor girl fled. The devil chased her and just as he was about to catch hold of her and with no help to hand, she stopped to make a desperate appeal to heaven for salvation. Instantly she was transformed into a column of lifeless granite and, according to tradition, she stands on that very spot to this very day in the form of the Maiden Stone at Drumdurno.

The column is, of course, much more likely to have Pictish origins and archaeologists agree that the 10½ft monolith is likely to date to from the ninth century AD. But occasionally, just occasionally, on a moonlit night some claim to have seen the devil himself wandering around in the nearby woods pining for his lost prize.

ꙮ ꙮ ꙮ

Gight Castle near Methlick, also known as The House of Gight, is one of the lesser-known castles of Aberdeenshire. Built in the fifteenth century by the Gordon family, it was for a time the home of Lord Byron's mother, until debts

The Maiden Stone at Crowmallie. (© Duncan Harley)

incurred by her husband, 'Mad Foulweather Jack', a conspicuous gambler and Coldstream Guards Officer, forced the sale of the castle and the estate. Nowadays only rooks inhabit the ruins and sheep graze around what should have been the Byron inheritance.

Lord Byron, of course, spent many of his formative years living in both Aberdeen, where there is a commemorative statue of the man, and elsewhere in Aberdeenshire. Alongside the Byron connection, legend has it that the ruins of Gight are haunted by a phantom piper who disappeared while exploring an underground passageway. The ruins sit high above the River Ythan and when the wind blows, his ghost, although rarely seen, can be heard playing the pipes under the ground. There are also dark tales suggesting that some of the castle's previous inhabitants dabbled in witchcraft and that the devil himself still visits the castle policies.

The road up to the building crosses over the River Ythan near a deep pool locally known as 'Hagberry Pot'. Named after the hagberry trees that line the riverbank, the pool is said to be bottomless and full of treasure. In 1644 the House of Gight was besieged by a Covenanter army and the 7th Laird of Gight is said to have instructed his servants to hide the family silver in the pool. Once the threat diminished, the laird ordered a servant to retrieve the treasure. The unfortunate diver seemingly returned empty-handed and reported to his laird that he had failed in his mission because the devil himself was down in the depths guarding the treasure.

Gight Castle. (© Duncan Harley)

Here accounts differ. Some say that the laird had the poor man tortured until he preferred the wrath of the devil to death at the laird's hands. Other versions of the folk tale assert that the servant was simply bullied and cajoled into agreeing to make a further attempt to retrieve the hoard. Whatever the truth of the matter, he is said to have exclaimed, 'I'd rather face the diel himself, than face the laird of Gight,' before once again diving into the black depths of the 'bottomless' pool. Just minutes after descending for the second time, the diver's body, severed into four pieces and his bloody heart still beating, shot to the surface to the horror of the watching bystanders. The laird's jewels were never recovered. Local lore insists that, to this day, no one else has dared explore the Hagberry Pot and that the laird's treasure still lies in the depths guarded by Beelzebub himself.

The village of Kemnay is perhaps best known for its once-prosperous granite quarrying industry. Although nowadays the village serves mainly as a commuter town for the oil industry, the place at one time came under attack by Old Hornie himself.

Seemingly, many years ago, the local priest was particularly outspoken and was prone to tirades urging parishioners to strike the devil from their hearts and thoughts. He even went as far as to ban the very mention of His Satanic Majesty's name in the village. Now, Satan was not at all pleased and in a fit of rage he took to hurling boulders at the priest from the top of Mither Tap, a nearby hill. There is no record of any of the granite missiles actually hitting the holy man but a giant boulder in a field near the farm of Greatstone is popularly believed to have been hurled by 'Aul Smith' and another at the Glebe may be evidence of a near miss.

Victorian bard William Cadenhead recalls the incident in his ballad 'Devil's Stone of Kemnay':

But the ponderous rock came on and on,
Well aimed for Kemnay Kirk,
And cross'd it field, or cross'd it flood,
It's shadow gar'd a' grow mirk.
But the fervent prayers o' the haly priest,
And the power o' the sweet Sanct Anne,
They turned the murderous rock aside,
And foiled the foul fiends plan.
And it lichted doon frae the darkened lift,
Like the greedy ernie bird,
And there it sits in the Kirk Lands yet,
Half buried in the yird.

The hurling of boulders from North-east hilltops was not confined to Auld Nick however. Scottish revolutionary Sir William Wallace allegedly threw a 5-ton lump of rock from the top of Mither Tap as far as Barra Hill, a distance of some 6 miles. The stone is nowadays known as 'Wallace's Putting Stone' and lies towards the north side of the hill, due, no doubt, to the fact that although Wallace's aim was good his throw overshot the summit by several hundred yards.

∿ ∿ ∿

The devil is also fabled to have thrown a boulder at no less a woman than his own wife! Standing, yet again, on the summit of Mither Tap, he took aim but missed the poor wench, who was wandering around the village of Midmar frightening the locals at the time. The stone fell short and landed near Tillycairn Castle at Cluny. Historian Alex Inkson McConnochie records in his book about Bennachie: 'The credulous may yet see the mark of the Devil's hand upon it.'

## ⚜ DORIC ⚜

The Doric tongue of the North-east is perhaps one of the most distinctive of the regional dialects still in regular daily use in Scotland. Sometimes described as the beautiful language of the north, according to some academics, Doric is a sub-set of the Scots language. There is some debate about whether the Doric tongue is a derivative of the Scots language or simply a local dialect. North-eastern writer Norman Harper suggests that Doric is 'the dialect of Scots spoken in the North-east of Scotland'. Derrick McClure, an academic specialising in Scottish literature and language, is wont to say that 'Doric is not, and never was, a separate language. It is a form of Scots, though a very distinctive one. Many words used by Doric writers can be understood all over Scotland and are no less Doric for that.' The Scots Language Centre, in its turn, suggests that Doric is 'distinct at a regional level, certainly, but is still part of the Scots language at a national level'. It may, they say, be a rural or rustic language associated with the countryside, peasantry and working class. The idea of Doric as a specifically North-eastern phenomenon is, they suggest, perhaps a very recent one. The discussions and debates rumble on. Even the number of Doric speakers is subject to debate, with estimates ranging from 30,000 to many times that figure. Whatever the truth of the matter, Doric conversation is not for the faint-hearted. Classic phrases include 'foo's yer doos?', which literally means 'how are you?' Then we have 'a fousome guff', which means 'an awfully bad smell'. 'Fit like' of course means 'how are you?' and 'quines and loons' are 'girls and boys'. A not untypical conversation might take the following form:

Fit like ma loon, foo's yer doos?

Aye peckin awa. Foo's yerself?

Ah weel, tae be honest am black affrontit.

Fit wye?

Weel, ah wis chavin awa jist fine when oot o'the blue ma loon came doon
wi' a face like a skelpit airse, sayin the guff wis like tae mak him spew but
I fair thocht he'd chockit it back.

And?

He hidna. Truth is he'd spewed a' ower ma doos and now they're nae peckin.

Dinna worry yer heid. It'll come aricht!

The emergence of the oil industry as the mainstay of the Aberdeenshire economy
has, not unnaturally, led to an Anglicisation of Doric among the natives of the
North-east. Many commentators have pointed to the need to meet and greet
international partners using a readily understood common language in order to
secure Aberdeen's reputation as the oil capital of Europe.

To aid the process and provide visitors with a crash course in the mysteries of the
dialect, a Doric dictionary was produced for the benefit of delegates attending the
2013 Offshore Europe oil and gas industry exhibition in Aberdeen. According to
the organisers, around 2,000 copies of the dictionary were handed out to delegates
in the hope of instructing them on how to 'ken their toonser from a teuchter and
a funcy piece from a bowfin' buttery'.

# *E*

## ❧ ELECTRICITY ❧

Doune Kirkyard sits on a headland high above the sea at Macduff and among the many gravestones is the family plot of one of Macduff's most celebrated residents, Aberdeen-born Dr Walford Bodie (1869–1939).

Sometimes known as the Laird of Macduff, he was variously billed as 'The Electric Wizard of the North' and 'The Most Remarkable Man on Earth'. A talented magician and illusionist, Bodie was never a man to shy away from publicity. An early career with the National Telephone Company gave him a good understanding of electricity and, over the course of a career spanning several decades, he astounded audiences by discharging thousands of volts of low-amperage electricity from his fingertips, in the form of bolts of lightning, before inviting members of the audience to step right up and take a seat in his electric chair. No doubt having flicked a switch to up the amperage, Bodie would then proceed to electrocute the unsuspecting volunteer before enthusiastically

The Bodie family plot at Doune Kirkyard. (© Duncan Harley)

reviving his blue-lipped subject with several hard slaps about the face, much to the amusement of the audience.

At the time, it was common practice for showmen to adopt the spurious title of Doctor and Bodie quickly added the letters MD to his name, but never publicly revealed what the letters actually meant. Some sources claim that in 1919, Bodie accidentally electrocuted his glamorous assistant, La Belle Electra, during a performance in Glasgow and she lies buried in the Bodie plot at Macduff. However, recent evidence casts doubt on this assertion and a distant relative has evidence that the woman in fact died of natural causes.

Even today, mention of the name Walford Bodie elicits memories. Maud resident Avril Wilson recalls a family tale about the man:

Auntie Fanny often spoke about how Uncle Jim went away on his bike to Bodie's concert at Mintlaw Hall. It was the 1920s, I suppose, and Bodie was touring all the local halls in the North-east. While he was off watching the performance, she gave birth to twins and Jim missed the birth. Bodie was quite a draw, you see.

Besides being a big draw, Walford Bodie was a high earner. Alongside the Manor House, on Macduff's Skene Street, he owned London properties, including a nightclub, several hotels and a houseboat on which he entertained celebrities, including Edward VIII and Wallis Simpson.

Dr Walford Bodie's manor house at Macduff. (© Duncan Harley)

He enhanced his income by endorsing 'electric ointments', including electric life pills, electric dentifrice and electric liniment. Today's trading standards would have had a field day. Generous to his adopted town, Bodie sponsored Macduff Walford FC, financed the local public baths and funded the Tarlair golf course. He was first to tee-off on the opening day in 1926.

A fountain in memory of his daughter, Jeannie, stands in Macduff's Maritime Memorial Garden, alongside the Peter Anson memorial sculpture. Known as the 'Bodie fountain', it was gifted to the town by the Bodie family in 1910, a year after Jeannie's death at just 19, and bears the poignant inscription: 'Drink, thirsty soul, and thank God.'

## ❖ ESPIONAGE ❖

During the early years of the Second World War, spies and saboteurs were put ashore all around the UK coastline, often by flying boat and sometimes by submarine. Usually they were quickly picked up by police suspicious of forged documents and in at least one case due to cycling along on the wrong side of the road. Spies making landfall on the Aberdeenshire coastline had a particularly difficult time of it since, due to the close-knit nature of the coastal communities, any stranger instantly came under special scrutiny.

During April 1941, two armed men landed at Crovie Pier from a rubber dinghy. Road signs had been removed in the North-east and the Emergency Coastal Defences were in place. General Ironside's nearby Innes Links Coastal Gun Battery was yet to fire a shot in anger, but the general mood was characterised by fear of invasion from German-held Norway and deep distrust of German-sounding foreigners.

The two men were dropped off a few miles offshore from a German flying boat around 3 a.m. on 8 April. They had lost some of their equipment while climbing into their rubber dinghy when the Luftwaffe aircrew, fearful of being caught on the surface by Allied air patrols, panicked and threw the men's bicycles into the North Sea, where no doubt they lie to this day.

As they watched the seaplane take off for the return trip to Norway, the pair must have wondered what on earth had possessed them to volunteer as German spies and what fate would await them when they made landfall. They were, in fact, Norwegian. John Helge Moe and Tor Glad had been recruited by the German security services to report on the Moray coastal defences and carry out acts of sabotage on the Scottish mainland. On disembarking at Crovie Pier the would-be spies seemingly knocked on the door of a local man and asked him in broken English how to get to Banff by bus.

Crovie harbour. (© Duncan Harley)

Very few locals spoke a foreign language and despite a recent influx of Italian prisoners of war and Polish servicemen into the area, the householder became suspicious and in due course the two men came to the attention of the local police. The luckless spies were promptly arrested and interrogated at Banff Police Station before being turned and used as double agents against their German masters. One later joined the Norwegian Army in Exile while the second lived out the remainder of the war in an internment camp.

In an effort to fool their German handlers and fend off any suspicion that they might have changed sides, MI5 apparently arranged fake sabotage operations that were then reported as the work of the pair. One such operation ended in farce when MI5 operatives were caught planting dummy incendiaries at a Ministry of Food's flour warehouse in Wealdstone. The investigation into this fake act of sabotage was quietly dropped by Scotland Yard but the plan had the desired effect since the incident was widely reported in the British press.

The two Norwegians are remembered locally by their MI5 codenames 'Mutt' and 'Jeff', a reference to a then popular American newspaper comic strip created by cartoonist Bud Fisher about 'two mismatched tinhorns'.

## ⚜ EXPLETIVES ⚜

Broadcaster Richard Dimbleby was a close friend and colleague of Robin Duff, the 32nd and last Laird of Oldmeldrum. Aberdeenshire-born Duff inherited both his lairdship and Meldrum House, the ancestral home, from his uncle in 1954. A Cambridge graduate, he worked as a presenter and then as a radio journalist for the BBC. During the Second World War, Robin famously stood on London rooftops during the Blitz, describing in graphic detail the Luftwaffe's bombing of the city.

In an interview conducted two years before his death, in 1990, aged 75, Robin recalled his long and distinguished career. He had covered the liberation of Europe, reported from the Normandy beaches during the Allied landings and been shot at by a sniper during the liberation of Paris. Post-war, he returned to France to record the Radio Scotland series *Duff's War*.

He was perhaps the very first newsman to broadcast an expletive on the normally sedate BBC Radio news. While reporting on the Blitz, his recording van was strafed by a German plane, which he said 'would have machine-gunned all of the reporting crew given the chance'. He quite naturally let loose with a few choice strong words that, after careful consideration, the news editors at the BBC and the wartime censors passed for broadcast.

On inheriting Meldrum House, Robin Duff turned part of the building into an award-winning hotel. Among a clientele that included entertainers, politicians and rock stars, a frequent visitor was ballet mega-star Dame Margot Fonteyn, a lifelong friend. Chairman of Scottish Ballet from 1973 until 1982, Robin co-wrote her autobiography.

Robin Duff is buried at St Matthew and St George's Episcopal church, Oldmeldrum.

Even today, the town of Banff would be familiar to the likes of Robert Burns and Dr Samuel Johnson, both of whom passed through during the latter part of the eighteenth century. Essayist Dr Johnson visited in 1773 and, on discovering that the Earl of Fife was not in residence at Duff House, was forced to overnight at a local inn, an experience he found quite unpleasant. His long-suffering travelling companion, James Boswell, records that the grumpy Johnson struggled to open the windows in his room and, on discovering that they had neither pulleys nor counterweights, commented that 'this wretched defect was general in the whole of Scotland … the necessity of ventilating human habitation has not yet been found by our Northern neighbours'.

## ❦ FABULOSITY ❦

Described by North-eastern journalist Jack Webster as 'quite simply one of the most gentle, kindly and considerate human beings I have ever known, a big, bearded, gangling Buchan loon', North-east-born fashion designer Bill Gibb left a legacy of his work in the permanent collections of many museums and art galleries throughout the world. London's Victoria and Albert Museum, New York's Metropolitan, Aberdeen Art Gallery and Zandra Rhodes's Fashion and Textiles Museum in Bermondsey, to name but a very few, have hosted retrospectives of his creations.

Born near New Pitsligo and schooled at Fraserburgh Academy, Bill showed a talent for design from an early age. Encouraged by his maternal grandmother, herself an accomplished landscape painter, and his art teachers at the academy, he went on to study at London's St Martin's School of Art and the Royal College of Art.

Fellow fashion students included Ossie Clark and Zandra Rhodes, with whom he shared an unbridled vision of what the Urban Dictionary likes to term 'fabulosity'. Indeed, years prior to the deconstructing of the kilt by the likes of Vivienne Westwood, Bill and fellow fashion designer Kaffe Fassett were creating the bold chequer board tartans and those wildly eccentric, richly mismatched knitted tartan and floral layers that came to symbolise the high fashion of the 1970s.

Bill's audacious and often wildly theatrical designs, replete with colour combinations such as lime green, purple, mustard and navy, soon caught on and by the early 1970s he found himself designing exclusive creations for the rich and famous. Roald Dahl's daughters wore his wedding dresses; Elizabeth Taylor, Bianca Jagger and Twiggy were among those who gathered wardrobes full of his designs.

Fraserburgh hosts the only permanent display of Bill's work in the UK outside of the V&A. Previously a foundry for the Consolidated Pneumatic Tool Company Ltd, known locally as the 'Toolies', Fraserburgh Heritage Museum is a must-see for those interested in the history of Fraserburgh and its folk. Bill's creations, bearing his signature 'Bumble Bee' motif, share museum space with extensive displays illustrating the life of 'Scottish Samurai' Thomas Blake Glover, the history of the local Marconi Wireless Shack at Broadsea, plus the varied career of local musician,

Fashion designer Bill Gibb montage at Fraserburgh Heritage Centre. (© Duncan Harley)

Charlie Chaplin lookalike and 'Chicken Hypnotist' Steve Fairnie; a man best-known, perhaps, as frontman of the post-punk band Writz.

Bill's younger sister, Patsy Davidson, recently commented that 'the family are keen to keep Billy's memory very much alive'.

While posing for a photograph alongside a montage of her brother's life, created by the pupils of Tyrie Primary School, Patsy became concerned that her shoes did not match her outfit. The man famously described by fashion model Twiggy as her 'knight in shining armour' would probably have approved wholeheartedly of the clash of colours.

## ⁂ FOLLIES ⁂

The North-eastern countryside is littered with heritage in the form of architecture from the near and distant past. There are Roman marching camps, castles galore and, of course, a multitude of ancient stone circles and standing stones. Most of these structures were built for a purpose. For example, each night on the march, the Roman army constructed a temporary camp, complete with rampart and ditch, as a defence against attack while in hostile territory. Examples can be found at Durno and at Kintore. The castles and big houses were in many cases also defensive structures but in more recent times they became potent symbols of the wealth that the area generated through agriculture, inheritance and trade. Debate, of course, continues over the true purpose of the standing stones and stone circles. Places of worship and centres of mystical ceremony, say some. Others wonder if the circles were simply settlements. After all, folk in those distant times needed a place to live.

Then, of course, there are the follies. There are various definitions describing follies, ranging from 'a structure with no practical use whatsoever' to the rather grand description 'a building constructed primarily for decoration, but either suggesting by its appearance some other purpose, or merely so extravagant that it transcends the normal range of garden ornaments or other class of building to which it belongs'.

Towers, cairns and temples seem to be the most common types of folly, perhaps due to their visual impact both on the landscape and on the visitor who chances upon them for the first time. However, some follies, such as the Shell Hoosie in Dunnotter Woods near Stonehaven, break the rules completely. Hidden deep within the woodland, the internal walls of this tiny domed building are decorated and completely covered with thousands of sea shells. Constructed by Lady Kennedy of nearby Dunnottar House in the early nineteenth century and restored in 1999, it has the appearance of a large beehive when seen from the outside but from inside it feels very much like a hermit's cave.

In stark contrast, the Lower Deeside town of Banchory is overlooked by Scolty Tower, a 20m granite monument built in 1842 to the memory of General William Burnett who fought alongside Wellington in the Napoleonic Wars. Also known as General Burnett's monument, there is some debate as to whether this tower is a true folly due to its commemorative purpose, and local opinion is divided as to the structure's true status. Following decades of neglect, it was restored in 1992 at a cost of £20,000 by the Rotary Club of Banchory.

A similar tower on the Hill of Ysthie, just outside the village of Tarves, bears a plaque recording that the structure was built by the tenants of Haddo Estate in memory of the 4th Earl of Aberdeen. Known as the 'Prop of Ythsie', the red granite tower, built *c.* 1850, resembles a giant chess piece abandoned in rolling farmland. In days gone by a flag was flown from the top to herald the start of curling season at the nearby Haddo House Curling Club.

Legend has it that an inquisitive cow once made its way up the spiral staircase and made it onto the viewing platform at the top of the tower. Since the unfortunate beast was unable to reverse back down the staircase, a rope and pulley had to be installed in order to lower it back to earth. A slightly more macabre version of this tale alleges that the poor beast was slaughtered and butchered before being taken back down the narrow stairs in small pieces.

The Prop of Ythsie. (© Duncan Harley)

Then there is the intriguingly named Temple of Theseus at Mintlaw, which was constructed around 1835 in the grounds of Pitfour House. A real hidden gem of a folly, the building is a scaled-down version of the sixth-century BC temple of Hephaestus in Athens and occupies a waterside location on the shores of Pitfour Lake.

At one time, the estate of Pitfour at Old Deer was one of the largest and arguably one of the grandest estates in Aberdeenshire. Between 1700 and 1924, the six lairds of Pitfour variously improved, enjoyed and finally depleted the capital of an estate affectionately known as 'the Blenheim of Buchan' – a reference to the richly landscaped Oxfordshire estate of the dukes of Marlborough.

At its peak, the Pitfour estate controlled around 30,000 acres of the Buchan countryside. Amidst all the grandeur stood the elaborate Pitfour House, with its 365 windows, fifty-two rooms, four staircases and twelve exterior portico pillars. Additionally, there was a private racecourse complete with neoclassical stable block, a private chapel and even a riding school, which doubled as a ballroom for weddings and large social events.

Long, tree-lined drives, decorative fountains and sunken gardens completed the visitor experience. The elaborate Pitfour House is long gone, although many

The Temple of Theseus at Pitfour. (© Duncan Harley)

structures, including the Greek temple and the stables, survive to this day. Theseus, of course, was the heroic slayer of the Minotaur, a half-man, half-bull maiden-devouring monster that lurked deep within a labyrinth on the island of Crete. Using nothing more than a ball of string to trace his steps and of course a trusty sword, Theseus defeated the Minotaur and thus saved the young folk of Athens from being ritually devoured by the evil monster. The Temple of Theseus in Aberdeenshire probably has no claim regarding the housing of a Minotaur, but there is a basement area complete with splash pool in which it is said the late Admiral Ferguson kept his pet alligator collection.

## ⚜ GOLF ⚜

The golf course at Cruden Bay is situated 23 miles north of Aberdeen, 10 miles south of Peterhead and around two hours' drive from St Andrews – the 'Home of Golf'. The Cruden Bay Golf Club has evidence, in the form of a ballot box inscribed 'Cruden Golf Club 1791', that a nine-hole golf course existed at the nearby Ward Hill in the late eighteenth century. The current eighteen-hole course was designed by Old Tom Morris of St Andrews, and opened in 1899 as part of the recreational facilities offered by the Great North of Scotland Railway Company's baronial-style Cruden Bay Hotel. A shorter nine-hole ladies' course was also available for the use of hotel guests.

From the outset, golfers came from all over the world to play at Cruden Bay and the grand opening in 1899 was celebrated with an inaugural two-day open tournament with prizes totalling £120. Even today, although the opulent hotel is long gone, the course on the Cruden Bay dunes is ranked as one of the best in Scotland and has been listed number fifty-two in the world by *Golf Magazine*.

From the outset, The GNSR marketed Cruden Bay as 'the Brighton of the North' and made great efforts to attract the rich and the famous to the luxurious pink Peterhead granite, eighty-two-bedroom hotel. Only twelve hours from London by train, the hotel offered an ideal holiday destination for the gentry and *nouveaux riche*. However, despite initial success, neither the railway nor the hotel prospered for long. The railway line closed to passengers in 1932 and in 1939 the hotel was requisitioned by the military before being demolished shortly after the war.

Well-known guests included Jeremiah Coleman of the mustard fame. In the 1970s a caddy by the name of Alexander Cruikshank who had carried the mustard tycoon's clubs, was interviewed for the *Scots Magazine*. He recalled that there were around 100 boys eagerly awaiting employment by the hotel caddy master and that at the start of the round the golfer was required to purchase a caddy ticket at a cost of 1 shilling. When the round was complete the caddy would customarily receive 9 pence as his payment.

Seemingly Jeremiah Coleman was in the habit of playing every day during his holiday. On the last day, he would habitually request that his caddy for the week should carry his clubs into the hotel foyer and ask at reception for Lady Coleman. Her ladyship would then appear and 'with Sir Jeremiah hovering in the background, would thank the caddy, present him with a half sovereign if this was his first year; or a whole sovereign on subsequent ones'. After thanking the young lad, she would do what every Cruden Bay Hotel caddy dreaded and kiss him sloppily on both cheeks.

The hotel kitchen was staffed by French and Italian chefs and it was said that any delicacy demanded by a guest could be provided. Victorians, then Edwardians and finally Georgians would alight from trains at the Cruden Bay Railway Station to be met by the hotel's head porter, who would usher them onto one of the two electric tramcars which ran up and down the narrow-gauge track between the station and the hotel entrance.

Publicity brochures advised that 'every modern comfort' was available for guests' use, including electric light, a lift and, of course, bathing machines. The local coalman's horse was apparently hired to pull the bathing machines to and from the sandy beach.

The two tramcars that ran up and down the dunes were built by the GNSR at the railway works at Kittybrewster in Aberdeen; following the eventual closure of the hotel, both found new uses as summer houses in nearby Hatton. In 1988, some forty-eight years after they ceased operation, the rusting remains of the two sixteen-seater trams were recovered for restoration by the Grampian Transport Museum at Alford. The best-preserved pieces of both vehicles were used to create the single car that is now on permanent display at the museum.

The narrow-gauge rail line used by the electric trams was dismantled in 1941, ostensibly to be melted down to aid the war effort. Since we now know that much of the wartime scrap metal gathered to manufacture munitions ended up in landfill, there is speculation that the remains of the track may be buried somewhere amongst the dunes awaiting a reunion with the restored electric tram at Alford.

෬෨ ෬෨ ෬෨

Turriff Golf Club moved to its current site at Rosehall in 1924, the original ten-hole course at Hutcheon Park having suffered from shortage of space to expand to eighteen holes. Described as 'a perfect walking course, at just over 6,000 yards' and with a par of seventy, the eighteen-hole course sits alongside the River Deveron and boasts a par five number twelve hole that, according to the club, provides an ideal opportunity for 'long hitters to bring out the big guns'.

During the Second World War, Rosehall was home to the Ministry of Supply Flax Works, which processed locally grown flax into the raw material for linen, medicines and even soap. Indeed, folklore has it that part of the output of the

Rosehall factory ended up flying over Nazi-occupied Europe: a variant of the wooden-framed De Havilland Mosquito fighter bomber employed fabric made from flax as a covering for its airframe.

At its peak, the factory employed over 120 folk but the wartime project was not a great success. Although experts from Belgium were consulted, the rich, heavy soil at Rosehall was better suited to golf than to the production and harvesting of flax.

చి చి చి

In a strange quirk of fate, the 126-year-old Stonehaven Golf Club actually benefited from those dark days of 1940 when the prospect of invasion by hostile German forces loomed. Founded in 1888 and with dramatic short holes played over deep gullies along the top of steep cliffs, the Stonehaven course is described as 'a challenging cliff-top course lying on the Braes of Cowie, overlooking the North Sea'. The first fairway features the infamous 'Hitler's Bunker', which consists of a large bomb crater made by the young men of the Luftwaffe during an air raid on Stonehaven during August 1940. Originally 30ft wide by 10ft deep, the bunker is now much reduced in size, but is still a major talking point among members, who will also point to the fact that the course spans the Highland Boundary Fault. This geological feature not only divides Scotland from east to west, but also separates the Stonehaven course's thirteenth and fifteenth holes, obliging golfers to carry their tee shots over a wide chasm known to golfers as 'the Gully'.

చి చి చి

Described as 'a superb nine hole/eighteen tee private golf course', the Royal Golf Course at Balmoral Castle, the private summer residence of Queen Elizabeth II, has in recent years been opened up to the public for twenty-six days each year. Of course, visitors can only play the par sixty-seven course when Her Majesty is not in residence and reports suggest that would-be Royal Course golfers may have to join a waiting list running into several years. The Balmoral course was laid out in 1925 and, 4,825yd in length, meanders its way around cairns and monuments from Queen Victoria's reign before following the line of the River Dee. The club made headlines when US President Donald Trump was reported to have said that he was looking forward to playing golf with the queen at Balmoral during his proposed official state visit to the UK. Newspapers in the North-east were quick to comment on the presidential ambition with one headline reading 'The Queen invites the Donald to Tee'.

చి చి చి

Fraserburgh Golf Club lays claim to being the fifth–oldest club in Scotland and the seventh-oldest in the world. The club may even be the oldest golf club in the world still operating under its original name. Golf is first documented as being played at Fraserburgh, known locally as 'the Broch', in 1613. Kirk Session records reveal the case of John Burnett, who was chastised for 'playing at the gouff' on a Sunday, instead of going to church. As punishment, he was sent to the 'maister's stool for correction'. The club has recently published a notice inviting visitors to the club's forthcoming anniversary. On 14 April 2027, members plus invited guests plan to celebrate the Fraserburgh Golf Club's sestercentennial (250th anniversary).

Only a true 'Brochter' could have thought that one up!

## ❧ GRAVESTONES ❧

Graveyards across the North-east house the remains of British and Commonwealth war dead. Many, mainly aircrew, were killed in training accidents. Some died in combat defending the North-east from enemy bombers. A few of these cemeteries also contain remains of the German airmen who waged war on Aberdeenshire. A row of headstones at Old Dyce Cemetery provide a clue to the story of one German aircrew killed when shot down in flames during July 1940.

The day of 12 July 1940 was overcast. There was low cloud in the south of England, but it was sunny and bright over Aberdeen. It was just two days into the Battle of Britain and the North-east had been subject to air attack several times during the previous fortnight. Early in the war it had been assumed that north-east Scotland was relatively safe from aerial attack; however, the invasion and conquest of Norway in April 1940 changed all that. Raiders could, from then on, reach the coast of Aberdeenshire easily and often undetected. Typical targets were shipping, factories and harbours, all of which the Aberdeenshire coastline offered in copious quantities.

Mid-morning of the 12th, a flight of six Heinkel He 111H-3 light bombers took off from Norway heading west over the North Sea. The intended target was RAF Leuchars and the harbour at Dundee, and the Tay Estuary was the intended landfall. For some reason, however, plans were altered mid-flight and the bombers headed along the Aberdeenshire coastline in search of prey. At 12.45 p.m., the first bombs began to fall on the Hall Russell Shipyard, in Aberdeen's harbour area. There was no air raid warning and the first anyone knew was when around sixteen high-explosive bombs exploded in quick succession. During the attack, one of the German raiders became detached from the main group.

Three fighter aircraft from nearby RAF Dyce had been scrambled minutes after the first bombs exploded. Manned by pilots of Yellow Section 603 Squadron, they were led by Pilot Officer Caister. The Spitfires headed straight towards the

German plane that had become separated from the main attack force, with the intention of shooting it down. Sensing the danger, the German pilot headed out over the North Sea, only to be driven back inland by the pursuing fighters. For around eight minutes or so a deadly game of cat and mouse was played out over North-east skies.

It was lunchtime and hundreds of folk on the ground were able to observe the unfolding drama. Eventually, after receiving several bursts of machine gun fire and being targeted by some quite ineffective shots from the anti-aircraft gun crews at the coastal battery at Torry, which put the pursuing fighters at more risk than the intended target, the bomber burst into flames and, heading back inland and across the city of Aberdeen, began a slow but inevitable descent to earth.

Some at the time wondered if the pilot had tried to avoid crashing into houses on the way down but others guessed that he had probably been dead or injured at the controls, as perhaps was the gunner who continued to fire his machine gun wildly all through the final descent. Whatever the truth, we will never know.

The end came suddenly and violently. Well alight and quite out of control, the bomber smashed into the newly built Aberdeen Ice Rink, which collapsed in flames around it. None of the aircraft's four-man crew survived, although one was found halfway out of the aircraft escape hatch with his parachute strapped on. Strangely, a lady's shoe was found in the wreckage, perhaps the property of a wife or lover who would never see her loved one again.

In true Boys' Own rhetoric, the newspapers of the day reported a 'Thrilling Dog-Fight with Spitfires' and 'bullets rattling on our roofs like a sea of hail'. The official record of the episode is more subdued:

The German graves at Old Dyce Kirkyard. (© Duncan Harley)

9/KG26 Heinkel He 111H-3. Sortied to attack Leuchars airfield with harbour installations at Broughty Ferry, Dundee, as alternate. Shot down by Yellow Section No 603 Squadron (Pilot Officer JR Caister, Pilot Officer GK Gilroy and Sergeant IK Arber) over Aberdeen 1.10 p.m. Crashed and burned out at the skating rink in South Anderson Drive. (Ff) Lt Herbert Huck, (Bf) Gefr Georg Kerkhoff, (Bm) Uffz Paul Plischke and (Beo) Fw August Skokan all killed. Aircraft 1H+FT a write-off. This crew were buried in Graves 155, 150, 149, and 152 in the Old Churchyard at Dyce on July 16, 1940.

The man credited with the kill, Pilot Officer Caister, executed a forced landing near Calais three months later and spent the rest of the war in captivity. The identity of the owner of the lady's shoe was never established.

ॐ ॐ ॐ

*Blind Boy's Pranks* might not be the snappiest title for an epic poem, but that is exactly what Inverurie's weaver-poet William Thom (1798–1848) called his inaugural piece. The poem was first published in the January 1841 edition of the *Aberdeen Herald*, alongside editorial comment praising his 'natural genius and cultivated taste'. *Blind Boy's Pranks* includes the following verses:

Twas just whaur creeping Ury greets
Its mountain cousin Don,
There wander'd forth a weelfaur'd dame,
Wha listless gazed on the bonnie stream,
As it flirted an' play'd with a sunny beam
That flicker'd its bosom upon.

Love happit his head, I trow, that time
The jessamine bark drew nigh,
The lassie espied the wee rosebud,
An' aye her heart gae thud for thud,
An' quiet it wadna lie.
O gin I but had yon wearie wee flower
That floats on the Ury sae fair!
She lootit her hand for the silly rose-leaf,
But little wist she o' the pawkie thief
That was lurkin' an' laughin' there!

Born in Aberdeen shortly after Burns's death, Thom spent just four years living in Inverurie's North Street, having moved there with second wife Jean Whitecross in 1840, to set up shop as a handloom weaver at a time when the weaving trade was dipping into a severe recession. Much of his early life was spent working as a weaver in both Aberdeen and Dundee, and although poverty and near-starvation were to follow him to Inverurie, it was here, in the Garioch town, that he produced perhaps his finest written work.

Nowadays, the 'Inverurie Poet' is perhaps best remembered for 'The Mitherless Bairn', a poem inspired on overhearing the greetin o' a wean in an Aberdeen street. Apparently, 'a lassie was thumpin' a bairn, when out cam a big dame, bellowin', "Ye hussie, will ye lick a mitherless bairn!"' However, it was the publication of *Blind Boy's Pranks* in local, then national, newspapers that lifted William Thom from penniless obscurity and launched him into polite London society where, for a year or so at least, he associated with the literary and political giants of the day, including Dickens and Thomas Carlyle. He was, he records, 'soon dashing it in a gilded carriage through the streets of London'.

Patronage and profits from book sales followed but, as is often the case with sudden wealth, his success attracted fair-weather cronies who took full advantage of his good-natured hospitality until such time as the money and the gin ran out. His fortunes then declined rapidly and, heavily in debt, he returned north to die, virtually penniless, in Dundee.

His tombstone, in Dundee's Western Cemetery, erected by admirers in 1857, confusingly records his year of birth as 1788 rather than the more generally accepted 1798. Fortunately, his short-lived fame outlived him and a benevolent fund, set up to provide for his widow and third wife, Jean Stephen, attracted donations from both Charles Dickens and Queen Victoria, who generously contributed £10.

ᐁ ᐁ ᐁ

Two of William Thom's wives lie buried in unmarked graves at Inverurie's Bass Cemetery and the graveyard holds the remains of Mary Elphinstone, known locally as Mary 'Eerie-Orie' Elphinstone. The unfortunate Mary Eerie-Orie was once buried alive after being mistakenly pronounced dead following a short illness.

The story is told in many versions. In one, her distraught second husband rescues her when he hears her desperate cries for help coming from the freshly filled grave. In another version of the tale, the gravedigger spies a gold ring on the corpse's finger. He tries and fails to remove it by hand and finally resorts to cutting off the unfortunate corpse's finger with his knife, at which point the 'deceased' wakes up howling in pain. She then leaps from the grave and runs home to Ardtannes, where she lives on until 1622. A third version of the tale has her running home to the house of a former husband. Whichever version you prefer, there is no doubt that Mary Elphinstone was one of those rarities to have had the privilege of being buried twice.

The William Thom memorial plaque at the old cemetery at Inverurie. (© Duncan Harley)

HERE, 'WHERE CREEPIN URY
GREETS ITS MOUNTAIN COUSIN DON'
LIE JEAN WHITECROSS d.1840
AND JEAN STEPHEN d.1848
COMMON-LAW WIVES OF
WILLIAM THOM
THE INVERURIE POET
ERECTED BY THE ROTARY CLUB
OF INVERURIE
1991

Jamie Fleeman lies buried at Longside churchyard. Alongside the usual information one might expect to find on a gravestone are his last words, 'Dinna bury me like a beast.' Known far and wide as 'the Laird of Udny's Fool', Jamie was employed by a local laird who, besides paying him to look after his geese, looked upon him as a kind of family jester. Described as having a 'large round head with dull hair that stood on end giving the impression he had been scared out of his wits', Jamie is specifically mentioned in various publications including the *New Statistical Account of Scotland* of 1845:

No offence is meant by introducing here the name of an individual who had a county - if not a national - reputation, and whose printed memorabilia have gone through several editions. This was Jamie Fleeman, the Laird of Udny's fool, who flourished here about the middle of last century. His name appears frequently in the session's list of paupers and his sayings and doings have been a theme of wonderment to a generation or two.

There are countless tales relating to the man, including one where he exchanges greetings with a local dignitary who unwisely asks him where he is going one fine

Jamie Fleeman's grave at Longside. (© Duncan Harley)

morning: 'I'm gaun' to hell, Sir,' replies Jamie. Later in the day, the two meet again and the gentleman asks Jamie, 'What are they doing in hell today, Jamie?' Jamie replies, 'Just fat' there doun' here, Sir, is lettin' in the rich foulk an' keepin' out the peer.' Not content with this answer, the gentleman probes further: 'And what said the devil to you, Jamie?' Jamie's reply startles the man: 'He said nae muckle to me, Sir; but he wis' far sair' about you.' On another occasion, when condescendingly asked, 'And whose fool are you?' Fleeman famously answered, 'I'm the Laird o' Udny's feel. An wha's feel are ye?'

Jamie Fleeman died in 1778 at his sister's house at Kinmundy. His last words were: 'I'm a Christian man, dinna bury me like a beast.' Despite this, he was buried in an unmarked grave and it took eighty-three years for his last wish to be granted.

In 1861, a handsome obelisk was erected over Jamie's unmarked grave at Longside. The cost of the monument had been raised in Aberdeen by public subscription and many of the subscribers travelled to the graveside on inauguration day to pay homage to a man who, to this day, remains more famous than the laird who hired him as his fool.

Jamie Fleeman's gravestone plaque at Longside. (© Duncan Harley)

In a further twist, Bram Stoker refers to Jamie in his tale 'Dracula's Guest': 'there is nae sic another fule in these parts. Nor has there been since the time o' Jamie Fleeman – him that was fule to the Laird o' Udny.'

ᔆ ᔆ ᔆ

Philip Kennedy was buried at Slains churchyard at Collieston in December 1798. A notorious smuggler, Philip and his brother John were surprised by a party of excise men in the process of moving a quantity of smuggled gin from the shore up to a safe hiding place on the family farm at nearby Ward. In the ensuing fight both brothers received deep cutlass wounds to the head. The first to be injured was John, who received a blow on the forehead that pierced through his thick bonnet and left him helpless, blinded by the thick stream of blood running over his eyes and face. After wounding John, the customs men shouted out to Philip to surrender or else have his head severed from his body. Philip chose to continue the fight and, uttering a dark oath, one of the excise man laid open his head with one fell stroke of his cutlass.

Although severely wounded, he staggered to a nearby farm shouting, 'Murder! Murder!' at the top of his voice. On arrival, he sat down heavily on a chair in the kitchen saying, 'If a' hed been as true as me the prize wud ha'e been safe, and I wudna' ha'e been bleedin' tae death.' After which he groaned loudly and expired on the kitchen floor. The skull of Philip Kennedy has occasionally been turned up during later interments. Gravediggers can easily identify it by the deep cut of the excise man's cutlass. His brother John lived on for another forty years. He died in 1842, and to the very end of his life also bore the excise man's mark.

## ❧ HANGING ❧

Robert Burns appears to have thoroughly enjoyed his 1787 visit to Banff. After breakfasting with the rector of Banff Academy, a linguist and distant acquaintance of his friend William Nicol, Burns was treated to a tour of the town by 13-year-old academy dux George Imlach. Imlach recalled many years later, in an article published in *Chambers's Journal*, that the bard paid particular attention to the paintings of the exiled Stuart kings in Duff House's great drawing room.

Inspired by local tales recounting the November 1700 execution of James MacPherson, possibly the last man to be hanged at Banff, Burns composed the ballad 'MacPherson's Farewell', thus immortalising the final hours of the notorious outlaw who was sentenced:

> to be taken to the Cross of Banff from the Tollbooth there of where you now lye, and there upon ane gibbit to be erected to be hanged by the neck to the death, by the hand of the common executioner, upon Friday nixt being the sixteenth day of November instant betwixt the hours of two and three in the afternoon.

Prior to his hanging, legend insists that MacPherson played a final lament on his fiddle before being turned off, and popular belief insists that the town clock was put forward by fifteen minutes in order to silence the infamous fiddler before a pardon could arrive to reprieve the man. Perhaps the wretched outlaw had made the fatal mistake of playing out of tune. Whatever the truth of the matter, Burns obviously was quite taken by the tale:

> There's some come here to see me hanged
> And some to buy my fiddle
> But before that I do part wi' her
> I'll brak her thro' the middle.
> He took the fiddle into both his hands
> And he broke it o'er a stone

Says there's nae other hand shall play on thee
When I am dead and gone.
O, little did my mother think
When she first cradled me
That I would turn a rovin' boy
And die on the gallows tree.
The reprive was comin' o'er the brig o' Banff
To let Macpherson free
But they pit the clock a quarter afore
And hanged him frae the tree.

Today, some claim that the 'clock that hanged MacPherson' now graces the clock tower in the Moray town of Dufftown. There are even rumours that the clock may be in the Garioch town of Inverurie, leading to suspicions that Banff folk were at one time quite adept at selling off dodgy timepieces.

෴ ෴ ෴

James Graham, 1st Marquis of Montrose was born in 1612, on the high street site now occupied by the local Job Centre Plus in the Angus town of Montrose. As one of the first to sign the National Covenant at Edinburgh in February 1638, the marquis rose to prominence in a Scotland torn asunder by religious and civil strife. Outlining radical demands for change in Scotland's governance, the Covenant led to a bloody civil war and would ultimately lead James Graham to the gallows.

Following his sacking of Aberdeen in 1644, a portion of his army, led by Alexander Irvine of Drum, entered Montrose's hometown with the intention of seizing the town's two brass cannon. Meeting local opposition, the marquis's troops destroyed the artillery pieces and plundered the town before withdrawing north for fear of a counterattack.

In 1645, the Aberdeenshire town of Alford played host to what was perhaps the Marquis of Montrose's easiest victory. After his defeat of Sir John Hurry's forces at Auldearn in early May 1645, Montrose had confronted a Covenanting army under Lieutenant-General William Baillie near Keith, but had declined to engage due to what he judged to be an impregnable defensive position. At Alford, however, Montrose took up positions on Gallows Hill, overlooking the River Don. Placing his troops out of sight on a reverse slope, he exposed a small force on the crest in order to encourage Baillie's forces to advance. As expected, they did so, and Montrose, who held the high ground, sprang his trap.

Accounts of casualties vary wildly, some sources suggesting ludicrously that 700 Covenanters perished for the loss of a mere dozen of Montrose's force. Perhaps the figure of a dozen refers to high-ranking combatants only and ignores the fate of the common soldier. In a curious twist of fate, Thomas Watt, great-grandfather of steam engineer James Watt, fought on the losing side. There is a monument to the battle on Alford's Donside Road, and a broadsword found on the battlefield was, for many years, exhibited in Aberdeen's Marischal College Museum.

It did not end well for the unfortunate marquis. In 1650, following defeat at the Battle of Carbisdale, he was betrayed by a highland laird. He and the remnants of his army were made prisoners of the Covenanting army and during the long march south for trial in Edinburgh, they presented a sorry sight.

Captain General John Graham Marquis of Montrose, to give him his full title, had been reserved for special treatment by his captors and following many nights spent in the open, he was dragged, bound and in filthy rags, to a parish churchyard in Moray. There he was subjected to a thunderous sermon from the local minister, concerning the 'slaughter of the Amalikites and the hewing into small pieces of Agag, as described in the Book of Samuel'. When Montrose perceived the drift of the sermon, he replied simply: 'Rail on, Rabshekah,' before turning his back on his tormentor. Montrose, of course, was already aware that he faced a sentence of death. Indeed, less than two weeks later, the unfortunate marquis was hung from a gibbet in Edinburgh.

His journey to the scaffold was not without further adventure. While imprisoned overnight at Pitcaple Castle near Inverurie, he was encouraged by the lady of the castle to escape by crawling through the 'garderobe flu'. Accounts passed down over time suggest that it was not the thought of crawling through excrement that put him off, but more the fear that the castle's owners might be severely punished that set him against escape.

The Scottish Parliament had already decided his fate, and on his arrival at Leith on 18 May 1650, he was taken straight to the Tolbooth. A few days later he made the short walk to the gallows. After paying the hangman four pieces of gold, Montrose made an impassioned speech and was pushed off. He was just 38 years old when he died and his final words were: 'May almighty God have mercy on this afflicted country.'

The execution took place at three in the afternoon and Montrose's lifeless body was cut down three hours later. At the foot of the scaffold lay various instruments of butchery conveniently arranged alongside some small wooden boxes. These boxes were duly filled with the dead marquis's limbs in preparation for their journey to various locations throughout Scotland. His head was placed on a spike at the Tolbooth and his mangled trunk was unceremoniously buried in a cesspit at the Burghmuir. Aberdeen had been assigned a lower limb and the box containing the bloodied leg duly headed north. On arrival, it was discovered that an arm had unfortunately been sent by mistake but rather than return the gruesome relic for an exchange, the city fathers ordered that the arm of Montrose be displayed on a spike at the Justice Port.

The Marquis of Montrose
statue. (© Duncan Harley)

In a strange postscript, a decade after the judicial murder, the Scottish Parliament ordered a state funeral for Montrose in order to make 'reparation for that horrid and monstrous barbarity fixed on Royal authority on the person of the great Marquis of Montrose'. The head and torso were retrieved and word was sent to Aberdeen requesting the return of the severed limb. In May 1661, the nobleman's remains were reburied at Edinburgh's St Giles Cathedral. Whether the Aberdeen limb reached Edinburgh in time for the official interment is still a matter for speculation. Indeed, many historians doubt that the marquis was buried with any of his scattered limbs.

In a further twist, writer Stuart Reid records in his book *The Campaigns of Montrose* that: 'Even in death, Montrose was to prove troublesome.' Seemingly, during the siege of Edinburgh Castle by Cromwell's forces in 1650, a gunner tried to dislodge the severed head of the marquis, which still sat atop a spike high on the Tolbooth. He missed his target entirely but brought down a lump of masonry that killed an unfortunate English drummer standing below.

## ❧ HERCULES ❧

In his 1791 poem 'Tam o' Shanter', Robert Burns recounts the tale of the drunken Tam who, wending his way home from the pub, chanced upon a group of dancing witches. Amongst them was Nannie Dee, whom Burns describes as being 'ae winsome wench and wawlie'. She wears a scanty linen *sark* that leaves little to the imagination and the sight of her dancing causes Tam to cry out, 'Weel done, Cutty-sark'. The resulting high-speed chase ends with Tam outrunning the pursuing coven. His horse, Maggie, is not quite so lucky and loses her tail to the pursuers in the final moments of the escape.

Burns famously had family connections in Aberdeenshire and visited more than once but visitors to Inverbervie are sometimes puzzled by the 10ft carved timber replica of the bare-breasted Nannie Dee at the entrance to the town.

Hercules Linton, designer of the super-fast tea clipper *Cutty Sark*, was, of course, born in Inverbervie in 1837 and the ship indelibly associated with him was launched in 1869. The original, restored at a cost of £25m following a disastrous fire in 2007, is docked at Greenwich.

The Inverbervie Cutty Sark Memorial.
(© Duncan Harley)

Hercules Linton was by all accounts a first-class marine designer; however, he lacked business sense. His first commission, for a small iron steamship named *Camel*, almost bankrupted him and his control of cash flow during the construction phase of the *Cutty Sark* was similarly dogged by problems. The contract for the vessel allowed for staged payment at the rate of £17 per ton of completed ship but only up to a maximum of 900 tons, after which there would be no further payments. In addition, failure to complete by the agreed date would incur heavy financial penalties.

Things did not go well. Although the clipper was eventually launched, some five months late in November 1869, Linton's business had by then collapsed. He eventually returned to Inverbervie in the 1890s and was elected onto the town council. Linton died in 1900 in the house he was born in, and is buried in the local churchyard.

A mystery remains as to why he suggested the name 'Cutty Sark' to the ship's owners since witches are legendary for being unable to cross running water. In fact, that is how the drunken Tam and his faithful steed Maggie make their escape in Burns's epic:

> A running stream they dare na cross.
> But ere the keystane she could make,
> The fient a tail she had to shake!
> For Nannie, far before the rest,
> Hard upon noble Maggie prest,
> And flew at Tam wi' furious ettle;
> But little wist she Maggie's mettle!
> Ae spring brought off her master hale,
> But left behind her ain grey tail:
> The carlin claught her by the rump,
> And left poor Maggie scarce a stump.

Hercules Linton must have had good reason for his choice of name though, and even when the ship was purchased by a Portuguese shipping company in 1895, and renamed *Ferreira*, the crew affectionately referred to her as *pequiña camisole*, which translates as 'skimpy nightdress'.

ல௦ ல௦ ல௦

Sporting superstar Donald Dinnie was, in his day, a Hercules of a different kind.

For a brief period after the railway arrived in 1859, Aboyne served as the railhead for the Royal Deeside Line and played host to Queen Victoria. When the royals and their guests disembarked from the royal steam trains they often stopped over at the town's Huntly Arms, perhaps Scotland's oldest coaching inn, before travelling on by horse-drawn coach to Balmoral Castle. The Huntly Arms has another claim to fame in the form of a stained-glass window commemorating the 'world's strongest man', local strongman Donald Dinnie.

A nineteenth-century sporting superstar and consummate showman, Dinnie achieved international fame when, in 1860, he carried two giant boulders, with a combined weight of 733lb, across the Deeside Potarch bridge and back. Alongside a lucrative career touring the international athletic circuits, Dinnie reigned supreme as the Highland Scottish sporting champion between 1856 and 1876, as an all-round athlete. Variously titled 'the World's Greatest Athlete' and 'All Round Champion of the World', Donald entered into sponsorship deals and, later in life, even lent his name to the 'Donald Dinnie' heavy artillery shells being lobbed at the enemy at the Somme and Passchendaele.

In 1903, he endorsed Scotland's 'other national drink', when his image was emblazoned on bottles alongside a caption proclaiming: 'I can recommend Barr's Iron Bru to all who wish to aspire to athletic fame.'

In modern times, the-so called 'Dinnie Stanes' have been the subject of many articles and documentaries. Additionally, they have been subjected to the attention of a succession of strong men and women from across the globe keen to emulate Donald's famous feat by lugging the Dinnie Stanes across the Potarch Bridge.

Indeed, the Dinnie legend still fascinates sportsmen the world over, and alongside regular local attempts to recreate the strongman's legendary feat, there are international competitions in which athletes attempt to replicate the lift. One

The Dinnie Window at the Huntly Arms Hotel in Aboyne. (© Duncan Harley)

such event took place as part of the 2017 Arnold Schwarzenegger Festival in Columbus, Ohio, where 'Regular World Strongest Man' Mark Felix won the lift and hold competition with an impressive 31-second lift of two replica Dinnie stones specially shipped over from Aberdeenshire. In truth, of course, the claim that the world's strongest man carried the stones across the Potarch Bridge is misleading since Dinnie actually carried them across the width of the bridge and not the entire length of the structure.

In his sporting career Dinnie took part in around 11,000 sporting contests and won over 150 sporting championships. Aberdeen Art Gallery holds a collection of Dinnie memorabilia, including many of his medals. Dinnie died in London in 1916. Fond of a whisky and a wager, he had drifted from sporting superstar to penniless pauper.

∽ ∽ ∽

Billed as 'Apollo the Scottish Hercules', Banff-born strongman William Bankier began his performing career early when, at age 12, he ran off to join the circus. Born in 1870, he got his big break when, during a spell working in a Canadian circus, he understudied the strongman. As the tour progressed and the strongman began to miss performances due to a love affair with the bottle, Bankier found himself taking over the lead spot.

During his subsequent career he added wrestling, boxing and jujitsu to his repertoire and began to build an international reputation as a stunt man. In one of his most famous death-defying stunts he allowed a car full of volunteers from the audience to run him over. In another act he lifted a full-grown man with his right hand and juggled plates with his left while balancing on the back of a chair.

Bankier went on to publish a bodybuilding guide entitled *Ideal Physical Culture and the Truth about the Strong Man* and after his retiral from the stage he opened a gymnasium in London. Later he became a leading wrestling promoter and in 1919 was elected 'King Rat' of the show business charity the Grand Order of Water Rats. He is perhaps best remembered for his 'Tomb of Hercules' feat of strength, in which he balanced a grand piano, topped with an entire six-man orchestra plus a scantily clad dancer, on his back.

The 'Scottish Hercules' died in 1949 in a Cheshire nursing home.

## *J*

## ❖ INDIANS ❖

Shortly after 5 a.m. on Tuesday 30 August 1904, several hundred curious onlookers watched a trio of special trains from Peterhead pull in to Fraserburgh railway station. The assembled crowd must have been agog as an army of strangely clad men and women began to unload the contents of the boxcars before proceeding down Dalrymple Street towards the Links. Dozens of horse-drawn wagons, piled high with circus tents, eighty mounted Lakota Indians in traditional dress and a contingent of blue-liveried US Cavalry led the way. They were closely followed by columns of Cuban patriots, South American *gauchos* and Mexican *vaqueros*.

On arrival at the Links, the cortège set about assembling a vast tented village complete with side shows, stables, carpenter's shop and even a smithy. The *Fraserburgh Herald* reported the 'marvellously quick way that the greater part of the Links was transformed into a canvas village' and commented on the 'enormous number of visitors' who had arrived from nearby towns such as St Combs, New Aberlour and Rosehearty. Billed as 'POSITIVELY THE FINAL VISIT TO GREAT BRITAIN' and 'AN INTERNATIONAL CONGRESS OF THE WORLD'S ROUGH RIDERS', the 800 performers and 500 horses of Buffalo Bill Cody's Wild West Show had arrived in town.

Always alert to the prospect of free publicity, Buffalo Bill Cody arranged a photo shoot on the South Pier. The images, which were later sold at 5 shillings apiece, show the grey-bearded showman atop his white charger alongside a posse of Native American warriors flanked by fishing boats of the local herring fleet. The Red Indians were then photographed at Kinnaird Point before being whisked off by publicists to tour the McConnachies canned herring factory, where they were each presented with a can of McConnachies finest pickled herring.

The first performance of the day began at 2 p.m. on the dot, the start of the big show was signalled by a single bugle note. The Cowboy Band then marched into the arena playing 'The Star-Spangled Banner' to an audience of 10,000 or more; then the event of the century began with a series of stirring pageants that, although perhaps lacking in historical authenticity, must have represented something

Buffalo Bill Cody and Lakota warriors on the South Pier at Fraserburgh. (Courtesy of Fraserburgh Heritage Centre)

of a culture shock to the assembled audience of townsfolk, farm workers and fisher folk.

With Colonel William F. Cody atop his white charger directing proceedings, a century or so of sanitised US history was re-enacted for the benefit of the folk of the Broch. The Deadwood stagecoach was ambushed, Custer's last stand was restaged and the Battle of the Little Big Horn was re-enacted. No spectators were reported shot, but Native Americans were slaughtered by the hundred.

Somewhat oddly, one of the biggest draws of the show was billed as 'The Intrepid Cowboy Cyclist in his Wonderful Bicycle Leap through Space' – a precursor to modern-day stunt motorcycling perhaps?

Following the evening performance, the show village was quickly dismantled and loaded carefully onto the waiting trains for the short journey south to Huntly where, the next day, the entire performance was repeated in front of another North-east audience. Following the Huntly performances, a Native American Indian performer by the name of Little Bear had to be left behind for treatment at the local cottage hospital due to a foot infection. He was to rejoin the Greatest Show on Earth at Perth a week later; but not before he had taken Huntly by storm when he attended Sunday service at St Margaret's Roman Catholic church on Chapel Street dressed in full costume and warpaint.

ᘒ ᘒ ᘒ

An Indian from an entirely different continent features in the strange tale of Queen Victoria's relationship with Hafiz Mohammed Abdul Karim. Visitors to Balmoral Castle in Upper Deeside are often unaware of the history of Karim Cottage. The picturesque timber–clad building overlooks the water garden and, when not occupied by members of the Royal Protection Unit, it is available as a holiday let. The original cottage, known as Garden Cottage, was a wooden building intended for the use of an estate gardener, although two of the rooms were set aside for Queen Victoria to take breakfast, deal with correspondence and maintain her diary.

By 1894 the building had fallen into disrepair and was demolished. The present replacement stone cottage was completed in 1895. Victoria's special relationship with her kilted manservant John Brown is well known. Many books have been written on the subject and some go so far as to claim that the pair were actually manservant and wife. Less well known is the tale of the monarch's affection for a man known by unkind members of the Royal Household as 'the brown Brown'.

Abdul Karim was just 24 when he arrived from India to wait at the royal table in 1887, four years after John Brown's death. The monarch was then 68. Karim had entered the royal household as a 'gift from India' and within a mere few months he was promoted well beyond ordinary servant status and had become a close confidant and regular companion to the head of the British Empire. He was soon given the title of Queen's Indian Secretary, a promotion, over the heads of longer-serving servants, which scandalised the royal household and enraged members of the royal family.

A set of official royal photographs taken by Aboyne photographer Robert Milne only made things worse. Taken inside Karim Cottage, they appear to show a diminutive Victoria, pen in hand, examining royal correspondence with a rather smug-looking Karim standing in the background. One picture, published in the *Daily Telegraph*, was captioned 'The Queen's life in the highlands. Her Majesty receiving a lesson in Hindustani from the Munshi Hafiz Mohammed Abdul Karim.' On the face of it, there was nothing to suggest impropriety and in fact the portrait clearly reflected an impeccably correct mistress and servant relationship. However, a storm of indignation soon arose. Some detected a hint of a smile on the monarch's face and leapt to a tabloid conclusion. Others, such as the queen's personal physician, Sir John Reid, went into attack mode. In a personal letter to Karim, he informed the man that he was 'very low class and never can be a gentleman!'

When Victoria announced that she was considering a knighthood for Karim, her son Bertie, Prince of Wales, became apoplectic and urged Dr Reid to take more direct action. Reid did not mince his words and promptly threatened to have his royal patient declared insane. In a personal letter to Victoria he wrote that:

There are people in high places who know Your Majesty well who say to me that the only charitable explanation that can be given is that Your Majesty is not sane; and that the time will come when, to save Your Majesty's memory and reputation, it will be necessary for me to come forward and say so.

Needless to say, for once in her life, Victoria was forced to back down and Karim did not receive the promised knighthood.

When Karim returned to India following Victoria's death in 1901, the successor to the throne, Edward VII, ordered the burning of all papers relating to the episode. Abdul Karim died in his native Agra in 1909.

## ℐ

## ⊰ JOURNEYS ⊱

Dr William Gordon Stables (1837–1910) was an early but enthusiastic proponent of the caravan holiday. Famously, he was also author of possibly the first caravan holiday guide. *The Cruise of the Land-Yacht 'Wanderer': Thirteen Hundred Miles in my Caravan* is, perhaps predictably, an account of his 1,300-mile horse-drawn caravan journey around Britain. It was published in about 1886.

Described as a 'shed on wheels', his 2-ton, 30ft caravan came complete with a China cabinet and was pulled along by Captain Cornflower and Polly Pea Blossom – his two horses. Dr Stables was particularly taken by the Aberdeenshire coastline and, in one of many criminal attempts to murder prose, infamously described the town of Banff in glowing terms: 'I have discovered Banff ... it is by far and away the most delightful town on the coast ... the scenery all around would delight the eyes of poet or artist.'

Reviewers took a dim view of his travelogue and one even went so far as to describe it as 'a dull narrative with occasional attempts at elaborate description and fine writing which are not very successful ... A more expensive and uncomfortable way of spending a holiday cannot be imagined and the experiences of the author certainly do not invite the reader to imitate him'.

Dr Stables was to have the last laugh however. In 1907 he was elected as the first vice president of the Caravan Club, which, some 110 years on, still celebrates the maiden voyage of what it claims was the world's first purpose-built touring caravan.

∽ ∽ ∽

Fortunately, accusations of dull writing cannot be levied at *The Caravan Pilgrimage* by Peter Anson. A prolific writer, religious scholar and marine artist, Anson had many claims to fame and his prolific output of books and drawings combine to tell the story of his life in some detail. His 1938 publication *The Caravan Pilgrimage* is an account of a year-long 'pilgrim artist' journey by horse-drawn caravan from Datchet, by the Thames, around Scotland's North-east coastline and then back south to Datchet.

For several years, Peter had been contributing a weekly series of drawings to *The Catholic Universe* newspaper featuring Catholic churches all around Britain. Subscribers would write in requesting that the paper feature their local church and Peter would be commissioned to write an illustrated feature. The work involved constant travel by train; he hated road travel, which he found exhausting. One day, Peter simply decided to divest himself of his copies of both Bradshaw and the *ABC Railway Guide* and purchased a horse-drawn caravan. Since he knew nothing about horses, his next move was to advertise for a travelling companion who did. Out of almost 200 applications he chose young Yorkshire man Anthony Rowe who, with a lifetime's experience among horses, was also a qualified farrier. Along with two horses, Jack and Bill, they set off on the year-long journey around Britain, sketching churches and meeting folk along the way.

Around sixty of Anson's illustrations of the pilgrimage appear in the book of the tour, including sketches of St Peter's in Buckie, St Mary's in Portsoy and St Thomas's in Keith. Along the way, Jack and Bill enjoyed the privilege of overnight grazing in, among many unusual locations, the grounds of Huntly Castle and Buckie FC's park.

With the arrival of the Deeside Railway at Aboyne in 1859 and its subsequent extension to Ballater in 1866, tourists seeking out the romance of the Highlands flocked to Deeside in droves. Tour companies began to offer package holidays and the Deeside towns of Banchory, Aboyne, Ballater and Braemar began to capitalise on that royal connection.

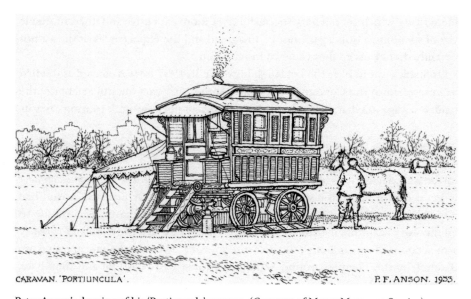

CARAVAN. 'PORTIUNCULA'.                                    P. F. ANSON. 1953.

Peter Anson's drawing of his 'Portiuncula' caravan. (Courtesy of Moray Museums Service)

Ballater station before the fire. (Courtesy of Cameron Davidson)

The railway never quite made it as far as Braemar, of course. The line was apparently surveyed but never laid much more than a few metres beyond Ballater, though a station was built at Braemar. Travellers made the final 17 miles of the journey between the railway terminus at Ballater and Braemar by road.

The station building at Ballater sadly burned down in 2015 but the original station building at Braemar still sits to this day beside the Invercauld Arms hotel, leading to confusion among hopeful visitors unaware perhaps that the brightly painted clapper-board building, with its hoarding proclaiming 'Great North of Scotland Railway', was simply the terminus for livery coaches and latter-day omnibuses.

In Queen Victoria's time, the royal train journey from Windsor to Ballater took two days and involved travelling 589 miles at speeds ranging from 25mph at night to 35mph during daylight hours. The locomotives of the day were quite capable of reaching speeds in excess of 60mph but the queen stipulated lower speeds due to her anxiety about the safety of this new mode of transport.

In the decades following Prince Albert's death at Windsor in 1861, the grieving monarch's constant companion John Brown was more than once seen on the footplate of the lead engine advising the driver that 'her majesty cannot gain sleep due to the rumbling of the locomotive at too much speed.'

The Deeside Railway closed to passengers in 1966 and tourists nowadays depend, yet again, on a tarmacadam version of the nineteenth-century turnpike road system.

∽ ∽ ∽

The railway network was instrumental in transforming Inverurie into a garrison town in the early years of the Second World War. In late May 1940, heavily censored news of the military disaster in France began appearing in newspapers across the UK. Headlines proclaiming 'Defence lines hold firm' soon gave way to 'Evacuation under bombs, BEF men arriving in thousands' as the retreat of the British Expeditionary Force from the beaches of Dunkirk began in earnest.

Despite continual German attack, some 338,000 Allied troops were ferried across the Channel to be disembarked at British ports between 27 May and 4 June. In the space of just eight days, 620 trains transported the exhausted and demoralised troops to towns throughout the UK for rest and re-equipping.

On 6 June, the citizens of Inverurie woke to find that the town had been invaded, not by the Germans, but by the British Army. In the early hours a train from Dover had disembarked several hundred hungry and demoralised soldiers, who now sat in dejected little groups all around the town centre, awaiting orders.

Fortunately, the town elders had been forewarned. Small groups of soldiers had been arriving piecemeal at the local railway station since 30 May, and billeting officers had been liaising with the Inverurie Church Council, who had wisely set up a canteen in the west church hall. However, the sheer scale of the invasion overwhelmed even the best-laid plans. As more trains arrived with even more troops, the local population and trades folk rallied to feed the bedraggled and exhausted army of stragglers.

Farmers sent milk and eggs; bakers and grocers emptied their shelves without thought of payment; local housewives, despite the burden of wartime rationing, baked till the cows came home.

The 'invasion of Inverurie' lasted about a week and, as many of the re-formed units moved on to outlying towns such as Huntly and Turriff, the crisis abated. However, due to the efficiency of the rail network, Inverurie had become a garrison town almost overnight.

৩৩ ৩৩ ৩৩

Known locally as 'The Mannie', Oldmeldrum's sailor boy statue is a well-travelled life-size stone sculpture of a mariner in period costume, which nowadays stands proudly outside the Meldrum Arms hotel on South Road. Rumours abound regarding his provenance. Few know his true origins and some even claim that Spanish gold lies buried beneath his feet. Originally, he held a clay pipe in one hand and a small anchor in the other. Clad in the style of a nineteenth-century French sailor, he is sculpted from Portland stone, the same material as Whitehall's Cenotaph.

Mysteriously, many years ago 'The Mannie' is said to have been purchased by Alford's Postie Lawson, inventor of the steam-powered Craigievar Express, at a

The Mannie at Oldmeldrum. (© Duncan Harley)

local farm sale for just 5 shillings. It is a fact confirmed by Grampian Transport Museum, which states that the statue stood outside Lawson's house at Craigievar until 1938, when it was relocated to Oldmeldrum.

If the Portland stone claim is accurate, before taking up residence at Oldmeldrum, the old salt may have made his way to Aberdeenshire via Dorset, where he is rumoured to have been commissioned by the widow of a drowned seafarer.

A Grade C listed statue, Oldmeldrum's Mannie would no doubt appreciate being reunited with the missing bowl of his clay pipe, which he appears to have lost along the way.

ᕮᕽ ᕮᕽ ᕮᕽ

The following notice appeared in *The Times* on Wednesday, 23 May 1945: 'Surrendered U-BOAT at Westminster Pier. The U-776, one of the German submarines which were surrendered at Weymouth is now moored to Westminster Pier, close by the Houses of Parliament, and will open to public inspection tomorrow.' This official notice from the Ministry of Information signalled the start of a UK tour like no other before it. When the war in Europe ended in May 1945, the Allies gained control of some 156 U-boats that had been ordered to make their way to the nearest Allied port to surrender. Most would eventually be towed out to sea to be sunk as part of a joint operation between the Fleet Air Arm and the Navy. A small number, perhaps thirty, of the more modern U-boats would be divided up between the victors and two of them would sail around the UK coastline in what the authorities chose to term an 'exhibition cruise'.

U-776 was chosen to tour the east coast and after a ten-day stint at London's Westminster Pier, the boat headed north. In mid-August, following a stop at Dundee, she sailed past Stonehaven, Newtonhill and Cove Bay on her journey towards the harbour at Aberdeen. Just a very few months before, the sight would have caused panic and have sent Coastal Command aircrew into a frenzy of activity. But because the war was over and, instead of a German pennant, a Royal Navy ensign now fluttered from the conning tower, the sight caused only mild interest amongst coastal spectators.

෯෨ ෯෨ ෯෨

In September 1787, as Robert Burns was nearing the end of his 600-mile 'vacation tour' of his native Scotland, he headed off to Stonehaven. Along with his travelling companion, Willie Nicol, he had left Edinburgh in May with the intention of collecting the national songs of Scotland as part of a collaboration with Edinburgh music publisher James Johnson. Armed with a satchel full of letters of introduction, they had dined and been wined by both lairds and cottars the length and breadth of the land and, by the end of the trip, had collected around 160 ballads for inclusion in Johnson's six-volume text *The Scots Musical Museum*.

Burns needed no letter of introduction upon arrival in Stonehaven, however, since his family had farmed at Clochanhill in Dunnottar Parish. During the short visit, he met up with his Mearns relatives before proceeding south to Laurencekirk and then Montrose. 'Near Stonehive [Stonehaven],' Burns writes in his diary of the trip, 'the coast is a good deal romantic. Met my relations. Robert Burns, a writer ... one of those who love fun, a gill, and a punning joke, and have not a bad heart, his wife a sweet, hospitable body, without any affectation of what is called town-breeding.'

Today, a civic garden alongside the River Cowie at Stonehaven commemorates the town's Burns connection. The centrepiece of the garden is a sandstone bust of the bard in classic pose, sculpted by local monumental mason 'Ghosty Bob'.

෯෨ ෯෨ ෯෨

In July 1914, Norwegian flyer and Antarctic explorer Tryggve Gran, the son of a wealthy Bergen shipbuilder, arrived at the Aberdeenshire coastal resort of Cruden Bay. He brought with him a number of large wooden crates containing

Robert Burns Memorial Garden at Stonehaven. (© Duncan Harley)

the dismantled components of a fragile second-hand 80hp Bleriot monoplane. His intention was to become the first aviator in history to make the perilous 320-mile flight across the North Sea to Stavanger.

By 17 July the aircraft had been assembled and all Gran had to do was await suitable flying weather. He waited and waited. Cruden Bay is, of course, completely exposed to the North Sea and a windy place even on the best of summer days. By the end of July, Gran had resorted to removing the plane's wings and lashing the fuselage to the ground in order to prevent the machine blowing away. He was under some pressure to get off the ground as soon as possible.

War in Europe was imminent and the British government had placed an embargo on all overseas flights from the UK after 6 p.m. on the 30 July, so the clock was literally ticking. Finally, early on 30 July 1914, a telegram arrived from Norway advising that flying conditions at that end looked promising and the intrepid Gran prepared his aircraft for take-off. At 8 a.m., narrowly missing the power lines that served the electric trams at the nearby Cruden Bay Hotel, the Norwegian took off from the beach and set course for Stavanger. His only navigational instrument was a compass and his sole means of judging wind direction was to observe the strength and direction of the waves on the surface of the North Sea far below.

An hour later he was back. Dense fog had made it impossible for him to see his compass in the open cockpit so he had made the decision to return and refuel. An hour or so later he was off again. The fog had lifted and after four hours in the air at altitudes of up to 6,000ft, he finally landed on the shore of a lake 20 miles south of Stavanger. The journey made history and his record-making flight over water stood until June 1919, when Alcock and Brown made the first non-stop transatlantic flight.

Tryggve Gran joined the Royal Flying Corps in 1916 under the pseudonym of Edward Grant, reputedly passing himself off as a Canadian. He is said to have received the Military Cross for distinguished war service. During the Second World War he attracted notoriety due to his membership of Quisling's pro-German National Party during the Nazi occupation of Norway. In 1944 a Norwegian stamp was issued to commemorate the thirtieth anniversary of his North Sea crossing.

Gran died in 1980 but returned to Cruden Bay in 1967 to attend a commemorative service at the local parish church. When interviewed and asked why he had chosen to risk his life on such a dangerous journey, he replied that he had chosen the route because he reasoned that by flying over such a busy shipping route, he would have a good chance of being rescued in the event that he had to ditch the plane.

A granite memorial in the shape of an aircraft propeller, commemorating the historic flight and made by students of Robert Gordon's College in Aberdeen, stands on the beachfront at Cruden Bay near the spot where Gran took off in 1914.

Tryggve Gran's Bleriot biplane. (Courtesy of Norsk Tecknisk Museum Oslo)

During the Second World War, the route taken by Gran was followed by the RAF fighter bombers of the Banff Strike Wing who, ironically, were tasked with raiding the Norwegian coastline in search of enemy shipping. The Strike Wing's primary mission was to disrupt German shipping and sink shipments of fish oil destined for use in the manufacture of explosives. At first light most days, a single reconnaissance aircraft, crewed by Norwegian airmen, took off from Banff's Boyndie Airfield closely followed by Mosquito fighter bombers, affectionately known as 'ship killers', whose job it was to sink the German convoys. Losses among aircrew were high and in 1989, a memorial to the eighty aircrew killed in action was unveiled on the Banff to Portsoy Road.

## ❧ KINGS ❧

If the tale of Peter Grant, better known locally in Braemar as 'Auld Dubrach', is to be believed in its entirety, the nineteenth-century travel writer Reverend Crombie's assertion that Braemar folk are blessed with 'unrivalled and disease-free longevity' may have some justification.

Born in 1714, the son of a local crofter, Peter joined the Jacobite army during the 1745 rebellion. Taken prisoner of war following the disaster of Culloden, he somehow escaped imprisonment at Carlisle and made his way home to Braemar, where he married and quietly resumed his trade as a tailor.

A curiosity, and possibly the last survivor from the final bid to restore the Stuart dynasty, according to folklore, Peter was presented to King George IV at the advanced age of 108 during the monarch's state visit to Edinburgh in 1822. When the pair met, the king reputedly said: 'Ah, Grant, you are my oldest friend,' only to receive the reply, 'Na, Na, your Majesty, I am your oldest enemy!' On further questioning regarding his Jacobite sympathies, Peter seemingly advised the king that he would again support the Stuart cause should the need arise.

Despite their obvious political differences, King George, thanks perhaps to the intervention of a sympathetic local laird, awarded Peter an annual pension of £50, which the old man received until his death, in 1824, at the quite remarkable age of 110.

Peter's gravestone lies close to the Farquharson family mausoleum in Braemar cemetery and the third fairway of Braemar Golf Club is named 'The Dubrach' in his memory.

⌀⌀ ⌀⌀ ⌀⌀

The town of Ellon lies some 16 miles north of Aberdeen and for centuries offered both friend and foe a convenient fording point over the River Ythan. In Roman times, the legions of Julius Agricola and Septimus Severus probably forded the Ythan at Ellon and in 1746 George Murray's Jacobite army also passed through the town on its long march north to support the Stuart cause at Culloden.

What impact the Romans and Murray's armies had on the town is unclear, but when King Robert the Bruce's armies arrived in 1308, the face of Ellon, and indeed the whole of Buchan, was changed completely. In what came to be known as the 'Harrying of Buchan', or the 'Herschip of Buchaine', Bruce's soldiers burned the town to the ground and put the population to the sword in a calculated and cruel move.

Virtually the whole of Buchan was laid waste by Bruce and his brother Edward. Farms, homes and crops were burned and livestock slaughtered. By terrorising the population, Bruce ensured that the folk of Buchan lost all loyalty to his enemies and a redistribution of former Comyn wealth to families such as the Hays completed the process. John Barbour, a Scottish poet and churchman (1320–1395), described the event in verse:

And gert his men bryn all Buchaine,
Fra end till end and sparyt nane,
And heryit thaim in sic maneir,
That eftre that weile fifty year,
Men meynt the hership of Buchaine.

Among the 17 million exhibits held by the Museum Victoria in Melbourne is a curious silver guinea dated 1716, but struck in 1828 by Mathew Young of London, probably from dies manufactured in preparation for what was intended to be a Scottish coinage for King James VIII. The British Museum holds a set of the original dies. The coin's face depicts the draped bust of James, the reverse showing four crowned shields, set to form a cross around a thistle, with the inscription *SCO AN FRA ET HIB REX 1716*.

Known as 'pretender coinage', the dies for the coins were made by Norbert Roettiers, a Paris-based engraver appointed by the exiled Stuarts. When George I was chosen to rule over Britain, in preference to James, many Scots were sympathetic to the Jacobite cause. Although James was recognised by his cousin, Louis XIV of France, as the rightful king of England, Scotland and Ireland, his refusal to renounce Catholicism made accession to the Protestant throne impossible, and the only course of action left to him was a military one.

A previous invasion in 1708, aided by France, had been thwarted before James could even set foot in Scotland. Seven years later, things would be different, or so he hoped. On 22 December 1715, the man who would be king landed at Peterhead. Crucially, he brought with him absolutely no guns or troops and, reputedly, no war chest. As if to emphasise his isolation, the French ship which delivered him to Aberdeenshire immediately set off back to Europe, fearful no doubt of ambush by English naval ships.

A James VIII silver guinea. (Courtesy of Museum Victoria, Melbourne)

Whether Peterhead was chosen by accident or design is not clear. However, in September 1715, the town had publicly made known its Jacobite sympathies via a proclamation for King James at the Mercat Cross. A meeting of the magistrates and town council on 5 October had concluded that due to the 'hazard and danger the Town may sustain by the inconvenience of the present times', a militia should be formed to defend the town. A gathering was called for 10 a.m. the following day, at which all the 'ffenceable men' were obliged to enlist and carry arms. In all, 138 men and ten women were issued with 'ane sufficient gun, charged with powder and bullets, and ffour shots besides, and ane sufficient suord'. In addition, cannon, reputedly salvaged from the wreck of the Spanish armada ship *St Michael*, were set up around the harbour mouth to defend the seaward approaches. However, when the prospective king finally arrived at Peterhead, three days before Christmas, thoughts of rebellion were already melting away.

The royal standard had been raised at Braemar on 6 September 1715, and the Scottish pro-Jacobite army, headed by the Earl of Mar, had marched on Perth. Indecisively, the key Jacobite battle at Sheriffmuir had been fought and seemingly lost by both sides on 13 November 1715. Dundee bard William McGonagall describes it thus: 'The success on either side is doubtful to this day, And all that can be said is, both armies ran away.'

Following further tactical withdrawals, James finally found himself at the port of Montrose on 3 February 1716, where he and the Earl of Mar boarded a small vessel and sailed for France. He never set foot in Scotland again. His dreams of rule in tatters, the would-be King James had spent just forty-three days on Scottish

Peterhead harbour defences. (© Duncan Harley)

soil and the sorry episode was to be repeated on a much grander scale during the disastrous rebellion of 1745, by his son Charles Edward Stuart, better known as Bonnie Prince Charlie.

Aberdeen Art Gallery and Museum houses a number of relics related to Bonnie Prince Charlie. These include a piece of red tartan said to be from his waistcoat and a piece of the mast of the ship in which the second failed Stuart pretender made his escape to the continent following the military disaster at the Battle of Culloden in 1746.

## ℒ

### ⁍ LEGENDS ⁌

Victorian writer and historian Alex Inkson McConnochie wrote several popular travelogues describing journeys in and around the hills and mountains of Aberdeenshire. One volume covers Ben Macdui, the second-highest mountain in Britain, while another describes that royal favourite, Lochnagar in Upper Deeside. Even today McConnachie's travel writings remain popular and much of the landscape he describes still exists in much the same form as in Victorian times. The wild places his words inhabit are largely unchanged, the history he describes is still relevant and the folklore he records remains the stuff of legends.

In his book about the Bennachie hill range, he dutifully records the route to the hill and, of course, the history of both place and people before launching the reader into the realm of legend. Bennachie has several tops, the highest of which is Oxen Craig at 1,733ft. The peak that stands out the most visually is Mither Tap at 1,699ft, and from its summit there are broad views across the entire county. People have scraped a living on the slopes for thousands of years and along the way they have recalled tales and passed on legends about angry giants and bewitching faeries.

Among the folklore associated with Bennachie is the story of two ploughmen who had the misfortune to meet some particularly malevolent fairies. McConnachie tells us that although 'Brownies, Spunkies and Kelpies were not unknown … Faeries were to be found and their music was to be heard everywhere about the hill and, as in other places, they were spoken of with respect by the inhabitants of the district.' Seemingly the fairies at Hill Park were particularly fond of playing 'sad tricks with the rustics'. The two young ploughmen were on their way to the smiddy one day when they came upon a group of fairies dancing and singing. Entranced at the sight, one of the young lads became transfixed and simply could not tear himself away. His companion quickly left the scene assuming that his friend would follow. However, the transfixed ploughman failed to appear and was not seen again for an entire year and a day.

McConnachie records that 'when his friend, passing by the same place, had his eyes so far opened as to see him standing, mouth open, intently watching something. On being asked to come along, he replied, as though he had only been there for a few minutes, that he would rather wait a little longer yet!' And there, seemingly, he still stands watching a faerie dance which no one else can see.

Legend also insists that the Bennachie of old was guarded by a giant known as Jock o' Bennachie. Proof of the existence of this giant exists to this day in the form of his enormous bed. Perhaps best known as 'Little John's Length', a plot of land to the east of the Bennachie peak of Craigshannoch, Jock's bed measures some 600ft from head to foot and indicates that he was pretty tall even for a giant.

Giants, of course, sometimes have enemies and Jock's nemesis was Jock o' Noth, who controlled the lands of Strathbogie and Rhynie. Jock o' Noth also lived on a hilltop, appropriately named Tap o' Noth, some 13 miles away. Petty squabbles over the affections of a mutually admired maiden occasionally erupted into full-scale war between the two giants and they sometimes resorted to chucking large boulders at each other. One such stone can be found somewhere on Tap o' Noth and apparently bears the giant handprint of Jock o' Bennachie.

When Jock o' Noth attempted to retaliate for this near miss, his adversary is said to have kicked the rock back into touch and to this day, they say, there is a boulder on Tap o' Noth that bears the mark of Jock o' Bennachie's big toe.

Of course, not all giant stories have a happy ending and Jock o' Bennachie appears to have fallen into a long, deep sleep while resting in his cave deep beneath the mountain. Legend has it that he will eventually wake up when someone finds the key to the door of his cave. He seems to have locked himself in by mistake. There are several ballads that celebrate the legends of the giants. One, which appears to be anonymous, appears in Inkson McConnachie's 1890 Bennachie guidebook and records that:

> An never sin' that awfu' nicht,
> Has Jock by mortal e'e,
> Been seen or heard o' far or near,
> Nor ever has the key.

In August 2013, a dramatic re-enactment of the battle between Jock o' Noth and Jock o' Bennachie was organised by the Bailies of Bennachie, a volunteer conservation group dedicated to caring for Bennachie and its landscape. Starting variously from Tap o' Noth or Mither Tap, two rival armies walked steadily towards each other, meeting approximately halfway on Suie Hill for a re-enactment titled 'the Giant's Throw'. While the original giant's throw involved lobbing great masses of rock across the 13-mile gap between the hill tops, the re-enactment used safer and more manageable softball weaponry. Participants were encouraged to keep a look out for the missing key to Jock's cave but, despite a good turnout on the day, no key was found and Jock is presumably still snoring softly in his cave.

## ⁂ LEOPARDS ⁂

In the pre-digital 1980s, Aberdeenshire boasted several publishing houses. Aberdeen Peoples Press (APP) was perhaps the best known and alongside printing radical political pamphlets, they enabled many local writers to make it into print. Long-forgotten publications such as *The Culter Courier* and *The Ferryhill Focus* were their bread and butter and the company, a workers' cooperative, published a fortnightly newspaper titled *Aberdeen Peoples Press*.

One of the cooperative's most infamous jobs was the printing of *Keltic Komics*, a satirical comic series penned by writers Dave Smith and Graham Murdoch. The magazine had a distinctly North-east theme, although titles such as 'Last Quango on Harris' and 'The Mystery of Auchnagoulash' conspicuously failed to make the *Times* bestseller list. In a brave attempt to sell all 2,000 copies, the authors set out on a desperate footslog around Aberdeenshire selling *Keltic Komics* from the back of an old pram to anyone brave enough to gamble a pound on their satirical prose.

Dave went on to write for theatre but Graham's career followed a quite different path. Under the pen name of 'Snoddy' – his pet cat – he created a comic strip for Viz. Titled 'Black Bag – The Faithful Border Bin Liner', the popular strip was a spoof of the DC Thompson Dandy comic strip 'Black Bob the Faithful Border Collie'. In the original storyline Black Bob helps shepherd Andrew Glen, his owner, round up sheep while also doggedly solving crimes, apprehending villains and generally doing good deeds. In the Snoddy version, an upper-class public schoolboy, accompanied by a black bin liner, wanders around the countryside generally messing up the lives of all the people he meets. In one infamous episode, he rescues 1976 Eurovision Song Contest winners Brotherhood of Man from a well and is callously killed as his reward.

෨෨ ෨෨ ෨෨

A stalwart from those heady days is *Leopard* magazine. Owned and published until recently by the University of Aberdeen, the publication has a long and lively history and was perhaps Scotland's very first regional magazine. The title *Leopard* is, of course, a reference to the heraldry of Aberdeen. The city's armorial bearings were granted around 1430.

Over the years since its first publication in August 1974, hundreds of writers, mainly local, have contributed to *Leopard*. Early content ranged from farming stories by Eddie Gillanders to Anne Tweedie's series on the then-emerging oil industry. North-eastern writer David Toulmin's 'Tillycorthy Story' and Ian Bryce's 'Castle of the Month' also featured.

for Aberdeen and North East Life

# LEOPARD
## Magazine
### 40p.

*An eighteenth century version of the arms
of the City of Aberdeen*

SEPTEMBER 1979

BON ACCORD

Bridge of Don ● Torry ● Dick Donald ● More Vanished
North East Mansions ● Sandy West and his Jazzmen
Victorian Ellon ● Cuthbert Graham ● Motoring
Cookery ● North East Weddings

*Leopard* magazine cover image. (© Duncan Harley)

Interviewed in 2014 by Judy Mackie, *Leopard* founding editor, Diane Morgan, recalled the early days:'Our material came from many unexpected sources,' she said:'For instance, after we complained about the quality of one of our bags of coal, the coal company's managing director came to visit us personally, and he told some marvellous stories about the old-time collier boats that delivered to Aberdeen.'

At *Leopard*'s fortieth birthday party, hosted by the University of Aberdeen's Elphinstone Institute in 2014, Diane recalled an early edition that featured a short story penned by a contributor under the pseudonym 'Disney Kerr'. Seemingly the writer, in reality a former postmaster residing in Portsoy, almost landed the fledgling magazine with an action for defamation.'All the characters were drawn from real life,' recalls Diane. 'No wonder we sold a lot of extra copies in Portsoy that month.'

The first issue of the magazine, besides featuring an editorial setting out the intent to 'provide a monthly diet of well-informed reading and exciting illustrations', included a free gift for readers in the form of a city map of Aberdeen. However, perhaps *Leopard*'s real secret to success can be seen in the inclusion of an advert extolling the virtues of an Aberdeen golf shop. Alongside some advertorial text inviting the reader to check out the shop's 'extensive range of colourful golf clothing' there stood a topless model.

That first-edition is, naturally, nowadays a sought-after collector's item and fans of the genre were probably disappointed to discover that in the facsimile edition of the first issue, reprinted for the fortieth anniversary celebrations, the model's bare breasts had been censored with a white bar strategically placed across her nipples.

## M

### ❧ MACBETH ☙

In a brutal act, central to that legendary Shakespearian play that cannot be named, King Macbeth was mortally wounded at the hands of his nemesis Malcolm Canmore in a bloody last stand on the outskirts of the Deeside village of Lumphanan. Although Shakespeare's play parts company on almost every detail of history, historical sites near where Macbeth fell, such as Macbeth's Stone and Macbeth's Well, attract large numbers of visitors each year eager to retrace the story of the Scottish noble. A prehistoric defensive structure known as the Lumphanan Peel Ring is said to be the actual location of the royal slaying.

In 1993, however, Lumphanan made the national news for a completely different reason when just 2 miles down the road, at nearby Torphins, three young men reported an encounter with a large, dark and very hairy figure that ran alongside their car as they drove into Aberdeen for a Friday night out. The hairy creature seemingly stared intently at the youths, and ran alongside the vehicle for nearly five minutes at speeds of up to 50mph, before suddenly vanishing completely. At around the same time, a local woman living in a secluded cottage reported sighting a giant, hairy figure lurking in the forest just outside her front door. There has never been a satisfactory explanation for the sightings although some wonder if Banquo's ghost had quite simply taken a wrong turn on his way to nearby Lumphanan.

෨෧ ෨෧ ෨෧

A hand puppet theatre group, the Scottish Sock Falcetto Theatre Company, made a mockery of the bloody murder of Macbeth during a performance at the Edinburgh Festival some years ago. Alongside comments such as 'Double, double toil and trouble; Fire burn, and caldron bubble', they pointed out that any mention of the word Macbeth on stage would expose Shakespearean actors to a lifetime of bad luck. In point of fact, though, the play contains quite a large amount of swordplay, so injuries to thespians are probably quite common.

Although unproven, there is strong suspicion that Shakespeare may have actually visited the North-east in 1601. Seemingly a playgroup known as the King's

Servants played at Aberdeen in that year and, albeit two years later, Shakespeare's name appears on a royal licence granted by James VI that sent players from the Globe Theatre off on a Scottish tour.

So, perhaps the bard who composed the Scottish Play had taken time out to gather some local knowledge of the murder of Macbeth.

## ⁂ MACDUFF ⁂

The planned township of Macduff has a relatively short history. As recently as 1759, the rent rolls for the settlement, known then as Down or Doune, recorded just thirty-four tenancies along with 400 inhabitants who subsisted on crofting and fishing from what was probably a very basic harbour. Today's population is around 3,850.

Burgh status came in 1783 and in that year the first town council sat down to deliberate on the improvement of the burgh. Markets were set up, vagrants were ostracised and residents forbidden to throw excrement and general rubbish onto the streets.

The earls of Fife invested heavily in the town and encouraged improvements in agricultural practices. They clearly understood the potential of exploiting the natural resources of the sea and began harbour improvements in the 1760s. The harbour has been upgraded at regular intervals up to the present day, with ownership passing from James Duff, the 2nd Earl of Fife to the town council in March 1897, for the 'nominal fee of £10,000'.

The Macduff Hollywood sign. (Courtesy of Dod Chalmers)

The second earl inherited the 'lands of Doune' in 1773 on the death of his father and within a few years, the thorny question of what to call his new town rose to the fore. In a letter to his factor, William Rose, dated 26 August 1781, he writes: 'If I change the name of Down, I would change it altogether and call it Macduff, as if we were to say *Down Duff*, wits would explain it as knocking *Down* my family.'

The canny laird must have had a sixth sense as well as a wry sense of humour, since, some 230 years later, a mysterious Hollywood-style sign spelling out 'MACDUFF' in 5ft letters unexpectedly appeared above the town, on top of Doune Hill. Over the succeeding two weeks, the giant sign successively morphed to form the words 'DUFFCAM', 'MADCUFF' and, finally, 'MACFFUD', at which point the local council felt obliged to enforce removal of the offending anagram.

The 2006 sign was the work of pranksters, but more recently a campaign group, convinced of the sign's marketing potential, gathered 2,059 signatures on a petition demanding its reinstatement.

The name Macduff is, of course, a reference to a Shakespearian character and the oft-quoted line 'Lead on, Macduff' is perhaps a Shakespearian misquotation. *The Illustrated Police News* of Saturday, 19 February 1898 reported that Joseph Callaway, 64, was fined 7 shillings for exclaiming in tragic tones: 'Lead on, Macduff, lead on! I'm the only real and genuine Sir Henry Irving.' Perhaps if he had shouted 'Lay on, Macffud' he would have received a much lower fine.

## ⚜ MEMORIALS ⚜

Scotland as a whole has an estimated 6,000 war memorials and in Aberdeenshire every town and village has at least one on display. Many more are dotted around the landscape at crossroads, local vantage points, inside churches and within public buildings. The Inverurie town square statue of a granite infantryman is a typical example of the genre, as is the roll of honour found within Insch Memorial Hospital in Aberdeenshire. The war memorial at Insch is built on land at Rothney given by the Laird of Leith Hall. It commemorates the war dead of Insch and the surrounding parishes.

Unusually for a community devastated at the savage losses during the conflict in the trenches, instead of building a simple granite monument complete with a list of the dead, the villagers raised funds by public subscription to build a cottage hospital. In total £7,500 was raised and the original hospital building was opened in August 1922. It housed eight general beds, three maternity beds and an operating theatre.

The lost sons of the folk of Auchleven, Old Rayne, Colpy and Insch are remembered on the carved wooden plaque in the entrance hallway. The casualty list for 1914–18 is particularly poignant, since the list of the dead records both name and parish, thus providing a stark picture of the localised impact of the conflict.

Insch War Memorial Hospital. (© Duncan Harley)

According to local GP Stephen Teale, early twentieth-century birth records reflected the devastating effect of the war on rural communities: 'The social effects were immense,' he says: 'The lack of available men meant that many local women never married and were left to run farms and crofts single-handed. The war had a tremendous impact ... there were also many men who returned injured both physically and mentally and unable to work.' Additionally, although few appreciate the fact, inheritance became problematic with farms changing hands simply because families had no young folk to take over.

The Insch Memorial Hospital has been variously extended through the intervening years since its opening. Although the original, rather modest building still lies at the core of the present building, it remains in daily use nearly a century on from its inception.

ൟ ൟ ൟ

Aboyne's war memorial sits in the Victory Hall on Ballater Road. Set in the heart of Deeside and officially known as the Aboyne and Glen Tanar Memorial Hall, the structure dates to 1920 and commemorates the dead of the Great War, of the Second World War and also those killed in the Korean War. The hall interior is in places quite grand and in particular the ceiling of the large main hall displays decorative open-timber purlins and trusses carved from massive trees felled in the local forests at Glen Tanar. In the Formaston Room is the Formaston Stone, an ancient Pictish cross slab stone with interlaced carving, a Pictish mirror symbol and an Ogham inscription.

Nowadays the hall plays host to weddings, Burns suppers and drama productions. A recent art exhibition featured the work of Potarch-based sculptress Helen Jackson, whose 3D willow sculptures of stags' heads hung, disconcertingly disembodied, side by side alongside the shot-and-stuffed genuine articles.

The entrance alcove to the hall sports a truly spectacular stained-glass panelled shrine commemorating those men who left Aboyne and nearby Glen Tanar during 1914–18, never to return. Unusually, an additional commemorative plaque displayed inside the main hall records the names of all those young men from the town and surrounding area who served in the Great War and returned alive.

∾ ∾ ∾

Muchalls is a coastal settlement to the south of Aberdeen. Described in the 1884 edition of the *Ordnance Gazetteer of Scotland* as: 'a village in Fetteresso parish, Kincardineshire, with a station on the North-Eastern section of the Caledonian railway, 5 miles NNE of Stonehaven, under which it has a telegraph and post office', Muchalls nowadays lacks a station but still sits alongside the main line linking Aberdeen to Edinburgh.

The Muchalls Peace Sign. (© Duncan Harley)

Charles Dickens is said to have described the village as a remarkably beautiful place and there are dark tales of a long-lost smuggler's cave, haunted by a green lady, linking Muchalls Castle to the nearby cliffs.

Today high-speed trains still pass through the village and sharp-eyed passengers might just snatch a glimpse of a concrete commemorative plaque on trackside embankment with the words 'Peace 1919' emblazoned on it.

The 20ft long memorial is locally known as the 'Muchalls Peace Sign' and was dedicated in August 1919 to commemorate the signing of the peace treaty between the victorious Allies and Germany on 28 June 1919. Designed by the then superintendent of Aberdeen's Duthie Park, the plaque was completed in record time by a local firm of plaster and cement merchants. Fittingly, perhaps, the use of cement for the plaque echoed the material used to build the original Cenotaph in Whitehall.

Edwin Lutyens's original timber and plaster Whitehall Cenotaph was hurriedly built as just one of a number of temporary ceremonial structures erected for the London Peace Day parade on 19 July 1919 and was only later replaced by the more permanent structure built from Portland stone that we see today.

The Muchalls Peace Sign was never upgraded and remains in its original form. Indeed, apart from an occasional makeover to remove weeds, the plaque is a tribute not only to those who lost life and limb in that war to end all wars, but to the undeniable durability of Aberdeenshire concrete.

# 𝓃

## ❖ NEMO ❖

*Nemo me impune lacessit* was the Latin motto of the Jacobite Pretenders. The motto translates as 'No one provokes me with impunity' or, in more direct language, 'Don't mess wi' me!'

In 1715 Braemar witnessed the raising of the Jacobite standard during the opening phase of the Stuart uprising. A secret meeting of Jacobite supporters had been held at Invercauld on 26 August of that year, at the behest of the Earl of Mar. However, the Laird of Invercauld, John Farquharson, was unconvinced that the timing was quite right for full-scale rebellion and asked if he could consider the matter for a few days. Accordingly, Mar headed over to Aboyne to consult with the Earl of Huntly, before returning to Braemar on 4 September, by which time Farquharson had decided to support the uprising. Two days later, the Earl of Mar

Raising of the Jacobite standard at Braemar. (© Duncan Harley)

raised the royal standard of James Edward Stuart in front of a Jacobite gathering of some 2,000 men at arms.

Tradition asserts that the richly embroidered flag bore the famous *Nemo me impune lacesset* motto plus the words 'No Union' alongside the Stuart royal arms and the thistle of Scotland. However, as the standard was raised to signal the rebellion, the gilt finial atop the flagstaff came loose and fell to the ground – an incident that many at the time considered a bad omen.

Subsequently, the Battle of Sheriffmuir on 13 November 1715 confirmed the portent. Although neither army gained the upper hand, this key engagement proved decisive in the defeat of the Jacobite cause. In *The Battle of Sherramuir*, Robert Burns writes 'Then ye may tell, how pell an mell, / By red claymores and musket's knell, / Wi'dying yell, how Tories fell, / And Whigs to hell, / Flew off in frighted' bands, man.'

Following the slaughter, Mar and his army retreated to Perth and the momentum of the uprising was lost. Despite plans for the coronation of the new Stuart king at Scone, it soon became obvious that the long-hoped-for uprising had simply fizzled out.

Accompanied by James Edward Stuart, the Earl of Mar escaped to France and, in February 1716, the remaining supporters received a message confirming his safe arrival and advising them to fend for themselves. Many Scots suffered imprisonment, execution and even transportation to the British colonies. Braemar suffered severely during the aftermath, when a vengeful government dispatched red-coated troops to the district with strict orders to burn crops and destroy property. When the government soldiers left, barely a house remained standing and the inhabitants were left with only blackened walls and ashes.

# ❖ NOVELS ❖

Visitors to the town of Huntly are sometimes puzzled by signs on the outskirts that read 'Huntly – Room to Roam'. Orb's Community Bookshop, in the town's Deveron Street, has an answer. Formerly a grocer shop, the building now houses several thousand pre-loved books. Pride of place goes to the works of local writer George MacDonald (1824–1905), whose writings appealed to a worldwide audience. He published around sixty works, including twenty novels, many set in Huntly. His popularity extended to all levels of society. When he was suffering from a lung complaint, Lady Byron gifted him an all-expenses-paid trip to Algiers to recuperate. Some years later, Queen Victoria presented her grandsons with a collection of his children's books.

Born in Bogie Street, where a plaque commemorates him, MacDonald is perhaps best known as the author of children's books such as *The Princess and the Goblin,* and fantasy novels such as *Lilith and Phantastes,* a 'Faerie Romance for Men and Women'. Cited as an inspiration for the likes of C.S. Lewis and T.S. Eliot, MacDonald's writings had an enormous impact on twentieth-century literature.

A poem from 'Phantastes – Room to Roam' was set to music in 1990 by Celtic folk-rock group The Waterboys, and in 2005, a line from the poem was adopted as part of Huntly's branding.

In a collaboration between Waterboys singer Mike Scott and South African artist Jacques Coetzer, MacDonald's poem was also developed into a town anthem, with a chorus reflecting MacDonald's work:

Room to roam but only one home
for all the world to win
So you go yours
and I'll go mine
and the many many ways we'll wend
Many days and many ways
ending in one end
Room to roam but only one home
ending in one end.

Perhaps MacDonald's greatest achievement, outside of his writing, was the admiration that other popular writers of his generation had for him. He was friendly with Mark Twain and Anthony Trollope. He was also on good terms with Ruskin, who seemingly confessed to him in remarkably intimate terms the difficulties of his tragic love life. Charles Lutwidge Dodgson, better known by his pen-name 'Lewis Carroll', was a particularly close friend and it was only after *Alice in Wonderland* had been tested out on the MacDonald family children that the bestselling book was finally sent off for publication.

৩৩ ৩৩ ৩৩

When John Reid wrote about his native North-east in his guise as David Toulmin, he penned some memorable stories. His tale 'Snowfire' springs to mind. Hitler's armies are at the very gates of Moscow and the Russians are fighting for their lives in the siege of Leningrad. It is 1942 and he records that the folk of Buchan were getting the 'tail-end' of the Russian winter 'so you dug the snow from the turnip drills ... and all you'd get for an afternoon's work was enough to fill a horse cart'. During a fierce blizzard, the farm's water supply freezes, leaving the drinking troughs empty. When the beasts are finally let onto the frozen river to drink from a hole in the ice, a German bomber appears overhead and the aircraft gunner sprays the ice with bullets, sending the thirst-crazed animals to a watery doom.

Not all of Toulmin's Buchan tales were quite as dramatic. In his social history piece 'Clarkie's and Aubrey's', published in his collection of stories *Straw into Gold: A Scots Miscellany*, he recounts the cinematic history of Peterhead. Seemingly a man by the name of Clarkie was the local ironmonger who, alongside studying the stock market, found time to run the Palace Theatre in Hanover Street. Previously known as the Electric Theatre, in earlier days it had been a skating rink. Unkind folk knew the place as 'the Bug Palace' since 'you sometimes got flechs' at Clarkie's'.

Up the road, in the main square, James Aubrey, another Peterhead entrepreneur, ran the Picture House, in the old music hall building. Described as 'a real posh place', it was the first variety house in Peterhead to convert exclusively to film, showing mainly love stories and newsreels. In 'Clarkie's and Aubrey's', Toulmin recounts the day, in the winter of 1926, when the Town House steeple toppled during a hurricane and fell through the roof of Aubrey's Picture House, much to the consternation of those who had just left the building after the evening performance.

Toulmin is nowadays internationally recognised as one of Aberdeenshire's finest exponents of the short story. Born on a farm at Rathen in Aberdeenshire, he worked as a farm labourer and spent most of his life working long hours on the land for very small rewards. In odd moments he jotted down short stories, character studies and bothy tales. Eventually, he had a few articles printed in local newspapers. The first of his ten books was published when he was 59. His literary output consisted mostly of short stories and reminiscences, his one novel, *Blown Seed,* painting a vivid and harsh picture of farm life as an indentured labourer.

In his later years, Reid moved to Pittodrie Place in Aberdeen, and later to Westhill. He was awarded an honorary Master's in literature by the University of Aberdeen in 1986 in recognition of his literary achievements. He died in 1998 aged 85 and Aberdeen University runs an annual short story competition in his name.

෭ඁ ෭ඁ ෭ඁ

James Leslie Mitchell was born in the village of Auchterless in 1901 and brought up in Arbuthnott. He took to writing early on and, in what was to be a very short career, produced some seventeen books. Perhaps the best known is *Sunset Song*, which he published in 1932 under the pen-name of Lewis Grassic Gibbon. It is a story of family tragedy, sexual depravity and heartbreak in rural Aberdeenshire, told from the stance of young Chris Guthrie, whose mother, her mind broken by repeated childbirths and learning that she is again pregnant, murders her baby twins and then kills herself. Torn between her love for the land and her desire to better herself, Chris endures further harrowing tragedies before eventually setting her sights on the local minister. Incest, a soldier shot for desertion and an unflinching picture of a brutal rural life set against the clouds of war feature strongly in the tale.

When it was first published, many readers expressed shock at the content. The realistic portrayal of childbirth and sex was one thing; but if truth be told, many of Gibbon's characters were alive and kicking and the name changes were a poor disguise for the guilty parties. The book upset many, including librarians, who in many cases, banned it from their shelves.

Despite the outrage caused by *Sunset Song*, Lewis Grassic Gibbon continued to pen books about the subsequent life of Chris Guthrie in the landmark trilogy known collectively as 'A Scots Quair'. *Cloud Howe* (1933) and *Grey Granite* (1934) were to follow and received various film, stage and TV adaptations.

Lewis Grassic Gibbon died at the early age of 34 in 1935 and the Lewis Grassic Gibbon Centre at Arbuthnott attracts visitors from all over the globe, keen to find out more about the author. Occasionally, however, staff report having to stifle a smile when visitors ask if they can visit the monkeys.

## ⁂ OUTRAGEOUS ⁂

Ellon Castle is a Category 'B' listed mansion house at one time owned by Dr James Reid, Royal Physician to Queen Victoria. After Victoria's death in 1901, Reid continued to serve the royal family, attending to both Edward VII and George V, before dying in 1923. The current building dates to 1724 and sits hidden behind a 12ft wall known as 'the deer dyke'. The ruin of the original castle stands nearby and the old building hides some dark secrets connected with a local laird sometimes referred to as 'the wicked earl'.

When Robert Burns visited Ellon in 1787, he recorded in his diary that he had intended to dine with George Gordon, 3rd Earl of Aberdeen, at the castle. Sadly he was denied entry and records: 'Entrance denied to everyone owing to the jealousy of *Three Score* over a kept country wench!'

The Bard's well-known reputation with the ladies had likely forewarned the vigorous old earl, who seemingly kept several mistresses in various local country retreats, including Ellon Castle. The scandal-ridden peer had sired children by at least three mistresses, in addition to the six borne by his long-suffering wife, Catherine Hanson. She apparently had been a humble cook from Wakefield before allegedly forcing him into marriage at gunpoint following his seduction of her. As for Burns, he simply recorded that: 'There is no such uncertainty as a sure thing.'

ᕫᕮ ᕫᕮ ᕫᕮ

When the railway arrived at Turriff in 1857, via the Inveramsay to Turriff extension, the project's shareholders anticipated good returns but, in truth, the line never became particularly busy and rarely turned a profit. A combination of competition from the Banff, Portsoy and Strathisla line and some 'recent deficient harvests' were blamed by the directors for the poor financial results.

The situation was probably not helped by the outrageous actions of the Turriff Post Office in sending the local posties up and down the line, carrying the mailbags as hand-held luggage, thus paying only a cheap day return passenger fare instead of the much higher cargo rates. As one local railway historian of the time commented: 'Turra folk hiv aye liked a guid bargain, an fit's wrang wi at?'

∽ ∽ ∽

The annual Meldrum Sports marked its eighty-fifth anniversary in 2015. Early events during the 1930s included a tug of war between single and married men plus various children's and adults' races. There is no record as to which team won the tug of war but the proceeds from the games were donated to a cocoa fund intended for the poorer children of the town. The year 1955 saw the first 'celebrity' opening of the games, when broadcaster Sir Richard Dimbleby opened proceedings in front of a record 15,000 people.

Currently part of the Glenfiddich Grampian Games Series, the 2015 event was opened by local resident and Commonwealth Games men's freestyle wrestling bronze medallist, Viorel Etko. Previous games have been opened by the likes of Jack Webster, Sooty and Sweep plus Aberdeenshire MP and ex-First Minister of the Scottish Parliament Alex Salmond.

In 1980, comedy revue team Scotland the What brought tears of laughter when comedian Steve Robertson played the part of Meldrum Sports Convener Sandy Thomson and made an impassioned spoof phone call to Her Majesty the Queen at Balmoral, inviting her to open the next year's event. The committee is still awaiting Her Majesty's official response.

∽ ∽ ∽

The Don bridge at Inverurie. (© Duncan Harley)

The original River Don bridge at Inverurie was completed by Banff mason James Robertson in 1791 and, despite powerful floods and the ravages of time, remained sound until the needs of twentieth-century transport forced its demolition to make way for a new crossing. The narrow roadway, plus the 7ft tall central hump that vehicles had to negotiate, had rendered the old bridge obsolete.

The contract for the new bridge was awarded to construction company William Tawse and, following the building of a temporary wooden crossing and demolition of the old bridge, construction of the new, reinforced concrete bridge began in April 1924. On the morning of 30 May 1925, an excited crowd of onlookers gathered at both ends of the newly completed bridge. At 10 a.m. a steam whistle blew and, with a mighty roar, two massive steam-driven road trains moved slowly in tandem onto the roadway. Each road train consisted of a steam-powered road roller towing two 8-ton trailers, plus a smaller 12-ton road roller and, as the engineers watched the vehicles' slow progress towards the north span, they must have wondered, at least briefly, if the design calculations and indeed the standard of construction would withstand the combined weight of the 92 tons of fire-breathing metal now heading straight towards them.

This was, of course, simply a load test; the official opening ceremony would follow three hours later. In a somewhat confident move, the load testing of the bridge, as required by the Ministry of Transport, was being carried out in anticipation of success.

Indeed, the scissors and ribbon that His Lordship the Rt Hon Earl of Kintore would use during the official opening ceremony were already to hand, as were the carefully prepared opening speeches.

The actual loads used were, however, somewhat lighter than those specified under the official testing specification, being a full 26 tons short of the required loading, which may, perhaps, have inspired the ambitious plan to both test and also open the bridge on the same day. Seemingly, heavier road rollers could not be obtained and two lighter machines were employed.

One of these rollers was an 18-ton French steamroller captured from the Germans in the latter stages of the 1914–18 war and bought by Tawse and Co. from the disposals board of HM Government. This leviathan had earlier proved its worth in the construction of the approach roads to the new bridge, and had also been used to test the temporary wooden bridge, constructed to allow passage of traffic, gas and water pipes during the construction period.

As the bridge engineers stood grouped around a depression gauge designed to measure the deflection of the roadway under load, they must have been relieved to record that the road surface lowered by a mere sixteenth of an inch, which increased to twice that when the road trains were later run across the bridge at full tilt.

Despite the quite outrageous flouting of the bridge-testing procedure, the official opening could now proceed as planned. Accordingly, at 1 p.m. that day, and to the rousing sound of the Inverurie Brass Band, the Earl of Kintore rose to make the opening ceremony speech. 'May this bridge stand for generations as a memorial to all concerned with its erection … I have now the pleasure of declaring this new bridge open for traffic.'

On being presented with a gold engraved cigarette case to mark the occasion by chief engineer William Tawse, the earl thanked the contractor: 'It is all the more appropriate, since, a few weeks ago, my rooms in London were burgled and among the things I lost was a gold cigarette case,' he said.

Despite the 'dodgy' testing procedure, the 90-year-old road bridge over the Don at Inverurie continues to give good service. As for the earl's stolen cigarette case, the crime remains unsolved.

## ❖ PICTS ❖

Long regarded as a lost warrior race of wild and naked blue-painted tribesmen who saw off the legions of Rome before vanishing from history forever, the ancient Picts did in fact leave a lasting record for all to see. They may not have taken pen to paper but the landscape of the North-east is littered with Pictish remains in the form of standing stones, many of which are elaborately carved. The Pictish period is generally reckoned to be between AD 300 and 900 and Aberdeenshire boasts around 20 per cent of the total number of Pictish stones recorded in Britain.

Discovered quite by chance in 1978 by a farmer ploughing his field, 'Rhynie Man' is a typical example of the genre. The 6ft tall stone bears a carving of a distinctively warlike figure with a large pointed nose and carrying an axe. Named Rhynie Man after the Aberdeenshire village in which the stone was found, archaeologists from the University of Aberdeen believe that the monolith dates to the fifth or sixth century AD and have nicknamed its figure Aberdeenshire's oldest man.

In 2015, an archaeological dig was carried out near the spot where Rhynie Man was discovered. Prior to the dig, Dr Gordon Noble, a senior lecturer in archaeology at the University of Aberdeen, commented that:

> Over the years, many theories have been put forward about the Rhynie Man. However, we don't have a huge amount of archaeology to back any of these up, so we want to explore the area in which he was found in much greater detail to yield clues about how and why he was created, and what the carved imagery might mean ... at more than six-feet high, the stone must have been an impressive sight to anyone coming to Rhynie some 1,500 years ago.

The dig featured a Pict-inspired pop-up café appropriately named Rhynie Woman. To date, there have been no reports of Rhynie Children being discovered in the vicinity.

The Pictish burial mound at Conyng Hillock is now little known and lies partially hidden in a private back garden near Kellands Park in Inverurie. In 1902 fragments of an urn were found at the site and charred wood was also dug up.

Tomb of Eth of the
Swift Foot at Inverurie.
(© Duncan Harley)

The only evidence of a burial cist was a fragment of stone lying at the foot of the hillock.

Local lore suggests that the 20ft high artificial burial mound is the resting place of Eth the Swift Foot, a Pictish king slain in battle nearby and buried at Inverurie in AD 878. Eth was seemingly named for his 'abnormal nimbleness of limb', enabling him to 'outstrip all his fellows in a running match'.

Clearly his extreme nimbleness failed to save him from death in battle. The jury is still out on the burial claim, however, since King Eth is also said to be interred on the west coast island of Iona.

ᕫᕬ ᕫᕬ ᕫᕬ

Described by archaeologists as a 'Pictish Cross-slab Ogham-inscribed', the Formaston Stone is sometimes referred to as the Aboyne Stone and sits within a protective glass casing in the Victory Hall at Aboyne. The ninth-century relic features several distinct decorative carvings, including a hand mirror, some finely interlaced Celtic knot work and a rare example of Ogham script.

The Formaston Stone took quite a while to get to its current destination and was originally discovered under the doorway of the old church of St Adamnan near Loch of Aboyne. During the nineteenth century the stone was apparently removed for safe keeping by the local laird and sat for many years in the private rose garden at Aboyne Castle. When the castle underwent extensive renovations in the 1970s, the Formaston Stone was moved to the (now closed) Andrew Carnegie Museum at Inverurie. Eventually, in 2002, the ancient stone returned to Deeside to be housed in Aboyne's Victory Hall where, thanks to the generosity of the

Marquis of Huntly and financial support from the Heritage Lottery scheme, the much-travelled relic remains on display.

ගෙ ගෙ ගෙ

As recently as 1974, a symbol stone bearing carvings of a double square, an elephant and a mirror was unearthed in Kintore and two carved stones, preserved when the Castle Hill was removed by railway engineers, now form part of the permanent collection of the National Museum of Antiquities of Scotland.

Another intricately carved Pictish symbol stone stands alongside the war memorial arch at Kintore parish church. Known as the Ichthus Stone, it is sculpted on both faces, the front bearing a fish and triple disc and bar symbols. The back of the stone bears a crescent and V-rod, plus carved elephant symbols.

Local author and occasional poet Reverend Dawson Scott wrote in his 1953 publication *The Story of Kintore* that the Ichthus Stone took up its present position in 1882 when the gravestones within the graveyard were put into rows. He records that 'when gravestones were set in line this stane wis pit aside the gate. A welcome frai the deid an' gane. This is God's Hoose, come pray, an' wait'.

## ⁑ PONDMASTERS ⁑

Several Aberdeenshire towns retain art deco buildings. At Stonehaven there are two superb examples in the form of an open-air heated swimming pool and the Carron restaurant building. Inverurie has an art deco hospital and although the site is under redevelopment to meet the needs of the twenty-first century, it looks likely that at least some vestiges of the original structure will be retained.

Tarlair art deco outdoor pool. (© Duncan Harley)

In other towns, the art deco heritage has sometimes been neglected and, in many cases, a lack of civic understanding has allowed architectural heritage to degrade to the point of demolition. The outdoor swimming pool at Tarlair, however, finds itself with a foot in both camps thanks to both an illustrious history and the efforts of the conservation group Friends of Tarlair.

Macduff was for many years a popular holiday destination, attracting visitors from all parts of the North-east and far beyond. The big attraction, of course, was the Tarlair pool. In the interwar period, around 169 such pool complexes, often known as lidos, operated at coastal resorts all around the UK, and the Tarlair Lido is one of only a very few remaining examples. Commissioned by Macduff Burgh Council, Tarlair Lido opened to the public in the summer of 1930, in partially completed form. Funding came via public subscription and from the government's Unemployment Grants Committee, a 1930s-style job creation scheme.

In 1935, the town council secured a £7,000 loan enabling completion of the ambitious project. Unlike the Stonehaven heated outdoor pool, Tarlair relied on the vagaries of the sun to warm the salt water. The main pool boasted a diving board and a chute, and there were paddling pools, a restaurant, sandpits and a large boating pond. The man in charge of the proceedings at Tarlair was known as the pondmaster. Swimming lessons could be arranged under his auspices and the pondmaster was in charge of health and safety. An eyewitness to Tarlair's glory days, Inverurie-born Anne Strachan, has mixed feelings regarding the attentiveness to health and safety of the Tarlair pondmaster however. As a child in the late 1940s she made the annual pilgrimage to Macduff by train with her family, before walking the mile or so to Tarlair. 'We went every summer holiday and took the train from Inverurie,' she recalls:

> My Uncle Dan would be in charge. He carried the pillowcase full of sandwiches, plus the small paraffin stove to heat the kettle. One year the stove must have leaked, so there was nothing else to do but eat the paraffin and cheese sandwiches.
>
> Another year, I nearly drowned when I came down the chute, and surfaced underneath a blow-up dinghy. Your family were supposed to look out for you, but mine took not a blind bit of notice! I don't think there were any lifeguards on duty in those days.

Tarlair's popularity waned in the latter part of the twentieth century. Closed to swimmers since 1996, the lido has been on the National Buildings at Risk register since 2008 and is now Grade A-listed. The site's owner, Aberdeenshire Council, recently completed a £300,000 refurbishment designed to stabilise the structure. Full reinstatement is likely to cost a further few million and the campaign group

Friends of Tarlair is actively fundraising with the intention of restoring the historic lido to full working order.

There have been various attempts over the decades to reinvent the Tarlair complex as a viable commercial concern. In the 1980s, with Woodstock firmly in mind, the pool was used as a concert venue and the pop group Wet Wet Wet famously landed a helicopter on the local golf course before performing in front of a crowd of several thousand.

Bizarrely, in more recent years there have been proposals to convert the pool to commercial use as an art deco lobster hatchery.

## ⁂ PRISONERS ⁂

Peterhead sits at the very easternmost point of mainland Scotland and even at the height of summer the town can be a cold and windy place. It is often referred to as 'the Bloo Toon' and the townsfolk are sometimes known as 'Bloo Tooners' of 'Bloomogganners' due in part to the cold blast of the winds sweeping in from the North Sea and also supposedly because of the blue worsted 'moggins' or stockings worn by the town's fishermen in times past.

The town today remains one of the busiest fishing ports in Europe and boasts a bustling daily fish market plus a 100-berth marina. It also has an Admiralty-designated harbour of refuge. Completed in 1956, following almost seventy years of construction, the harbour of refuge is one of Peterhead's most prominent landmarks, providing a safe haven for North Sea shipping in all weathers. To cut costs, it was decided early on to employ convict labour, and when construction began in 1886, the Harbour of Refuge Act provided for the building of a convict prison on the outskirts of the town, at Invernettie.

The use of forced labour was not a new idea. The Admiralty was involved in a similar project in Dover, using convicts from Langdon Prison. Aberdeenshire contractors MacAndrew & Co. began constructing the first cell blocks in 1886 and, on completion, these housed the captive labour force needed to build both the rest of the prison and the sea defences. A 2.5-mile narrow-gauge railway, at the time probably the only state-owned railway in Scotland, was laid between the Admiralty yard at Salthousehead and the granite quarry at Stirlinghill. The mammoth task of constructing the breakwaters then began.

Conditions were harsh. Civil guards were armed with rifles and prison warders wielded cutlasses. Despite the armed guards and high security there were escape attempts. In July 1932, for example, a Strichen man serving seven years for armed robbery was shot dead attempting to escape from the quarry.

Infamous Peterhead Prison inmates included Scottish sculptor, novelist and convicted murderer Jimmy Boyle and Glasgow gangster Arthur Thompson.

Less infamous were wrongly imprisoned innocents Paddy Meehan and Oscar Slater.

In 1918, the prison played host to the Scottish Socialist leader John McLean. A fierce opponent of the First World War, he was convicted of sedition and spent five months on hunger strike at Peterhead before being released in December 1918, as part of a raft of concessions following government fears of a Marxist Scottish revolution.

In 2013, Scotland's gulag, as the old Peterhead Prison had come to be known, was replaced by a modern, purpose-built £150m super jail capable of housing 552 men, women and young offenders, supervised by 360 staff. The days of forced manual labour are gone forever and in a programme designed to aid integration, inmates are now encouraged to learn call-centre skills. Perhaps next time you order a pizza or make a National Rail enquiry, the helpful voice at the end of the line will be speaking from a prison call centre in Peterhead.

One of Peterhead Prison's most celebrated prisoners was a man dubbed 'Gentle Johnny Ramensky' by the press. A skilled safe cracker and prison escapologist extraordinaire, Johnny Ramensky drifted into crime at an early age. The tag 'Gentle Johnny' came about due to his frequent habit of escaping from prison before surrendering to the police without any attempt at a struggle. He was to spend much of his adult life in prison and much of his prison life escaping from behind bars. He is said to have escaped from Peterhead Prison on at least five occasions, although during one evasion lasting five days he was in fact holed up in a cupboard within the prison walls.

In 1934, he escaped yet again from Peterhead and, in scenes reminiscent of the manhunt in John Buchan's novel *The Thirty-Nine Steps*, police set up roadblocks throughout North-east Scotland. Crofts and farms were searched and vehicles were stopped, presumably to check for suspicious-looking occupants wearing prison-issue garb. In a quite remarkable escapade, Ramensky managed to avoid a roadblock on a bridge over the Ythan at Ellon by edging hand-over-hand along the stonework underneath the roadway before slipping quietly away south towards

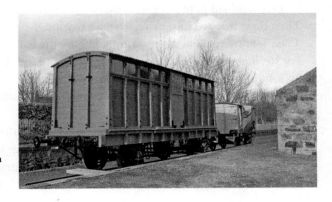

A restored Peterhead prison
wagon at Maude railway
station. (© Duncan Harley)

Aberdeen. Quite which bridge Johnny used to cross the River Ythan is uncertain, although most accounts point to the old road bridge at the foot of Bridge Street as the likely culprit. What is certain, however, is that he was later recaptured in a tattie field near Balmedie, 9 miles south of the town.

Johnny Ramensky was to repeat his trick of sneaking over the Ythan unseen some years later, before yet again being caught near Balmedie. In the intervening period, he had gained notoriety for breaking into an Aberdeen laundry and blowing open one of the two safes inside the building. In a letter dated 13 October 1938 intended for the prison review board, he wrote:

> I want to inform the proper authorities to remove a charge of gelignite which is inside the lock of the small safe. The police think that the explosive was used up but it was not … I had both safes ready for firing. I blew the big safe first and on searching it found the key for the small safe. So I put the key in the lock of the small safe and opened it. I could not get the gelignite out again because once in and round the lock it was out of sight.

The Aberdeen police were not amused. The gelignite-rigged second safe was, at the time, securely locked up in a police department strong room in Aberdeen city centre awaiting return to the laundry's head office.

Johnny Ramensky went on to serve his country as a demolition engineer during the Second World War, after which he returned to his old ways. A popular song about him, 'The Ballad of Johnny Ramensky', was written by Labour MP Norman Buchan and recorded for posterity by Scottish folk singer Hamish Imlach. The song includes the following lines:

> There was a lad in Glesga town, Ramensky was his name
> Johnny didnae know it then but he was set for fame
> But when the war was raging the brass-hats had a plan
> Tae purloin some information, but they couldnae find a man
> So they nobbled John in prison, asked if he would take a chance
> Then they dropped him in a parachute beyond the coast of France
> Then Johnny was a hero, they shook him by the hand
> For stealing secret documents frae the German High Command
> So Johnny was rewarded for the job he did sae well
> They granted him a pardon frae the prison and the cell.

Gentle Johnny Ramensky became ill in Perth Prison in 1972. He was transferred to Perth Royal Infirmary and died there on 4 November of the same year, having spent a short period of his life serving queen and country and the bulk of it as a guest of Her Majesty.

## ⚜ QUEENS ⚜

Author John Buchan once described Walter Scott's 1814 novel *Waverley* as a 'riot of fun and eccentricity', a view not shared by a great many other commentators. Some critics have even been known to view Scott's tales of wild tartan-clad Highlanders, romanticised castles and heroic Jacobite insurrection as somewhat dour, inaccurate and humourless. Notwithstanding, Sir Walter was charged with organising festivities for the 1822 visit of King George IV to Scotland in which 'the garb of old Gaul', the kilt and the tartan, featured prominently.

The royal romance with the Highlands had been kindled and decades later, in 1852, following some three years of careful negotiation, Queen Victoria and the Royal Consort Prince Albert purchased the by then run down Balmoral estate, the previous owner having died after choking on a fishbone. By 1856 the new Balmoral Castle was complete. The original building was completely demolished and Victoria's 'dear paradise in the Highlands' was good to go.

The 50,000 acres of the new and now 'royal' Balmoral estate attracted the good and the great to Deeside to hunt, shoot and fish and, in consequence, Royal Deeside flourished. Alongside the international figures and parliamentarians of the day, hordes of Victorian tourists flocked to the area by road and rail in the hope of both experiencing Walter Scott's romanticised Highlands and fitting in a bit of royal spotting.

Today, the queen and various members of the royal family spend much of August at Balmoral and, by tradition, many important guests are invited to wine, dine and hunt at the castle. But staying at Balmoral could, in the past at least, be something of an ordeal. The rooms, despite their delightful tartan-themed décor, were criticised by some visitors as being tiny, damp and quite cluttered. Lord Clarendon was one such critic. He famously wrote in 1856 that: 'Thistles are in such abundance that they would rejoice the heart of a donkey.' Marie Mallet wrote in the 1890s about the 'dreadful food and footmen reeking of whisky', and guests often complained that Victoria, a great lover of the outdoors, 'had the windows open while we were at dinner'. Some guests also objected to the 'whisky fuelled evenings of merriment and dancing around piles of newly slain stags', as depicted in Carl Haag's painting 'Evening at Balmoral'. Others, such as Liberal

Balmoral Castle.
(Courtesy of
Balmoral Estate)

Prime Minister Campbell Bannerman, simply hated the place: 'It is the funniest life conceivable. Like a convent. We meet at meals, breakfast, lunch, dinner and when we have finished each is off to his cell.'

In the twenty-first century, the Balmoral estate takes a more sanguine approach to criticisms of Prince Albert's architectural vision, stating only that: 'Although it remains largely the same as it was in Queen Victoria's reign, successive Royal owners have followed the initiative of Prince Albert in making improvements to the estate.' The building that tourists see today dates to the 1850s and is built in a style variously described as Scottish baronial or Scots Tudor. Designed to reflect the tastes of Prince Albert, the structure, with its great keep-like tower and turreted façade, is in fact more of a Germanic *Schloss* or family home than a Scottish castle. Victoria loved the place, referring to it as her 'Dear Paradise in the Highlands'.

Among Victoria's many visitors were folk such as Robert Peel, Benjamin Disraeli and William Gladstone, as well as a good selection of the crowned heads of Europe. Perhaps the most infamous, aside from Kaiser Wilhelm II, was Tsar Nicholas II who, with his wife Alexandra Feodorovna, grand-daughter of Victoria, visited Balmoral in the autumn of 1896. The local press reported that 'the heavens opened as in tears' when the Tsar alighted from the royal train at Ballater station in front of a waiting bodyguard of 100 drenched men of the Black Watch.

Leon Trotsky would later refer to the Tsar as 'more awful than all the tyrants of ancient and modern history' and Aberdeen's *Bon Accord* magazine seemingly agreed. A reporter from the publication penned an article criticising the visit, commenting that: 'When the Tsar is at home we do not hesitate to call him a tyrant. Then in heavens name, why then, when he visits his grand-mother-in-law should we play the hypocrite and fete he whom we at other times curse.' Some years later at a Russian town by the name of Yekaterinburg, the locals agreed with Trotsky and shot the Tsar dead.

ᨦ ᨦ ᨦ

Amid cheers from close family and curious onlookers and with a rousing tune from the Aberdeen Police Pipe Band, a tired but visibly relieved young woman emerged from isolation in Tor-Na-Dee Hospital, Milltimber, clutching a bouquet and wearing a brightly coloured sash that proclaimed her 'typhoid queen 1964'.

It was Friday, 19 June and, following a thirty-day ordeal, 23-year-old press librarian Evelyn Gauld had become the first of 500 patients being treated for typhoid to be discharged from the hospital after what is still remembered worldwide as the 'Aberdeen typhoid epidemic'.

This dubious title of 'typhoid queen' was a gift to the press, and headlines right across the globe proclaimed her 'the symbol of Aberdeen'. After more than four weeks of headlines dedicated to the plight of the beleaguered North-east, an end to the crisis was in sight and an official royal visit by HRH Queen Elizabeth II, nine days after Evelyn's discharge, seemed to confirm the county that had been described as a leper colony was now safe enough for royalty to travel through, albeit in a sealed limousine.

Dr MacQueen, the medical officer of health responsible for dealing with the outbreak, was holidaying in Wales when he heard about the queen's impending visit. He checked planes, trains and road routes, and found that the only way to get home in time to welcome the monarch was to drive full-speed to catch an overnight train at Crewe. Police cars from two counties escorted him all the way and he made the train. 'The police were tremendous,' he said. 'It was an exciting experience.' Strangely, perhaps, no one even thought to introduce the two queens and although press reports of the time make great play of both the typhoid queen's release from hospital and of the high-profile visit of the reigning monarch, they were destined never to meet.

ᨦ ᨦ ᨦ

In September 1562 Mary Queen of Scots set out on one of several tours around Scotland. Each of her tours, known as 'progressions', lasted for weeks at a time and in consequence she stayed at various castles and country houses along the way. Estimates vary wildly, but it is likely that at least eighty historic houses in Scotland can rightly make the claim 'Mary Queen of Scots stayed here' in their respective guidebooks. Some, such as Pitcaple Castle, can really only claim that the monarch visited briefly along the way. Seemingly Mary stayed overnight at nearby Balquhain Castle before taking breakfast at Pitcaple.

After her breakfast, the queen stayed on long enough to plant a thorn tree, which survived until 1856, when it blew down. It was later replaced by a red maple planted by a later Queen Mary, wife of George V, in 1923.

A model of Mary, Queen of Scots.
(© Duncan Harley)

In 1562 Mary was a spectator at the Battle of Corrichie near Banchory. The conflict had resulted from a dispute in which the Earl of Huntly came out against the queen. The earl's forces were soundly defeated but before he could be brought to justice, the unfortunate man died of apoplexy. His demise was summed up graphically by a witness who recorded that 'without either blowe or stroke he sodenlie fawlethe from his horse starke dedde!'

Many of the captured rebel leaders were executed and, even in death, Huntly did not escape punishment. His corpse was transported to Aberdeen Tolbooth, where a local surgeon was charged with embalming it. In February 1563, with Mary Queen of Scots in attendance, Huntly's by now putrefying corpse, was put on trial in Edinburgh and found guilty of high treason. The sentence was forfeiture of all of his lands and possessions. In 1566, when passions had cooled, the guilty corpse was returned to his family for burial at Elgin Cathedral.

As for Mary, she was beheaded in 1587 following trial and conviction for plotting against her cousin, Queen Elizabeth I. Her last words were 'In manus tuas, Domine, commendo spiritum meum' (Into thy hands, O Lord I commend my spirit), after which the executioner, in a supremely botched execution, drove his axe deep into the back of her head.

Among the exhibits at Blairs Museum on the outskirts of Aberdeen is a full-length portrait of Mary dressed exactly as she would have been on the day of her execution. Reproduced from a miniature smuggled abroad by one of her 'Mary's in waiting', the portrait was returned to Scotland many years after her death, having been saved from the mob during the French Revolution by being rolled up and then hidden in a chimneybreast.

## ⚛ RAILWAYS ⚛

For many decades, the Inverurie Railway Works was a major employer in Aberdeenshire. Occupying a 24-acre site and locally known as the 'loco works', the engineering facility was completed in 1905 to replace the Great North of Scotland Railway's cramped workshops at Kittybrewster in Aberdeen. To accommodate the labour force, workers' housing was built at what later became known as 'the Colony'. In those class-conscious times, the gaffers' houses were built to a standard superior to the tenements built for manual workers. However, all of the new colony houses boasted electric light courtesy of the loco's generating plant; this at a time when most Inverurie folk would have relied on gas or oil for both cooking and lighting.

Concentrating mainly on locomotive and rolling stock repairs, with only ten steam locomotives actually being built on site, the facility very quickly became the major employer in the town, with employee numbers peaking at 847 in 1946, out of a total burgh population of 3,960.

The factory closed on 31 December 1969, with over 500 job losses, but the legacy of the Inverurie Loco Works lives on in the form of sporting and social clubs, including Inverurie Loco Works FC. Formed in 1902, and now elevated to the Highland Football League, the club has played continuously throughout its 112-year history. Club historian David Fasken says the Locos were probably one of only two Scottish junior football clubs to play without interruption throughout the Second World War. 'Mind you,' he adds, 'due to wartime conscription, there were a few occasions when the team manager was forced to borrow a couple of Italian POWs from the camp next door to complete the team.'

Whether armed guards were in place during such matches is not recorded. However, the club grounds still sport a fine example of a Type 24 concrete pillbox, one of only two still surviving in the town, which no doubt would have deterred potential escapees.

⚯ ⚯ ⚯

The railway came late to the Garioch town of Oldmeldrum in the form of a 6-mile branch line from Inverurie. The line was officially opened with great fanfare in June 1856 and operated for 109 years until closure in 1965. The opening ceremony made headlines and was celebrated with a banquet in the new engine shed, where 300 invited guests drank a massive thirty toasts to the success of the new venture.

The eventual closure of the line also made headlines and featured on the BBC TV news, perhaps due to the romanticism associated with the line's locomotives. Seemingly Oldmeldrum's steam trains ranked high in the affection of the locals, who nicknamed successive engines 'Meldrum Meg'. This was down to Aberdeenshire humourist Dufton Scott (1880–1944), who for some now-forgotten reason had referred to an early steam locomotive as Meldrum Meg during a poetry recital. The name caught the popular imagination.

In 1931 the final scheduled passenger service ran on the line and the loss was lamented in the following verse:

Meldrum Meg has gone at last
An' her racing days are past
Nae mair ye'll hear me sing the auld refrain
So I think that me an' you
Should drink her health in mountain dew
For we'll never see anither like the Meldrum Train.

The Meldrum railway line continued to transport goods until 1965. In December of that year a small crowd gathered to watch the final cargo of 666 gallons of whisky from the Glen Garioch distillery leave for Inverurie.

In 2012 a heritage railway society purchased the Oldmeldrum station waiting room, which was built around 1890. Without much fanfare, they loaded the wooden building onto a truck and drove it the 30 miles or so to Milton-of-Crathes, where it now serves weekend passengers on the Royal Deeside Railway.

ဆ ဆ ဆ

In the 1870s, a war of attrition broke out between Pitfour estate near Old Deer and the neighbouring estate of Aden. Both landowners were burdened by debt and they had a long history of animosity. The first trains from Mintlaw to Aberdeen ran in July 1861 and the line to Peterhead opened the following year, followed by the Fraserburgh line a few years later. The railway line through Maud cut through both the Pitfour and Aden estates at various points and in some places parcels of land belonging to each had become completely cut off from direct access by their respective owners.

In 1875, the laird of Aden estate quite sensibly suggested that an agreement be reached to exchange land in order to sort out these anomalies. He proposed to exchange Pitfour land south of the railway for Aden land over at Kininmonth. Unfortunately, a dispute soon broke out regarding the valuation of the land in question and, despite independent arbiters being appointed, neither side would agree to abide by the result of arbitration. A long feud ensued. Aden closed off a country lane and thus blocked access to Pitfour land that had been cut off by the railway. In retaliation, the laird of Pitfour applied for an interdict to stop his neighbour draining disputed land. Between 1875 and 1887, the two lairds engaged in a petty litigation game involving water rights, salmon fishing rights and, at one point, even the course of the River Ugie. The only folk to gain were the lawyers.

The dispute finally ended after the death of the Aden laird, James Russell. His successor reached an amicable agreement with Pitfour in 1887. Approximately 611 acres of Pitfour land was exchanged for approximately 611 acres of Aden land with no money whatsoever changing hands. Common sense had finally prevailed and the bizarre war between the lairds of Aden and Pitfour was finally at an end.

## ❧ RIOTS ❧

The railway arrived in Stonehaven in 1849 and by 1863, *Bradshaw's Railway Guide* was describing the town as: 'The county town of Kincardineshire with a population of about 3,240 who are principally engaged in the herring trade fisheries, distilleries and breweries.' Bradshaw goes on to state that the railway station was 1 mile from the sea and that there was 'but one telegraph station in the town'.

However, on the fateful day of the Stonehaven Railway Riot of 5 January 1848 there appears to have been no working telegraph station in the town. The local constabulary, consisting of six constables headed by Superintendent of Police Alexander Weir, were completely outnumbered when faced with a drunken mob of more than 200 railway navvies. Some of the rioters were armed with pickaxe handles and the beleaguered bobbies had no obvious way to summon help.

The previous weekend, navvies had fought with locals and on this holiday weekend they had decided to take over the town. Windows were smashed, the Mill Inn suffered damage and passers-by were jostled and in some cases bludgeoned. After six hours of rampage, the mob dispersed and calm prevailed – but a local man, William Murray, lay dead, having been assaulted in Allardice Street.

The transcript for the Circuit Court of Justiciary for the County of Aberdeen, on Monday, 10 April 1848, records the punishment handed out to the usual suspects: 'George Keith, age 13 from Banff, guilty of burglary – 18 months in Perth Prison. Elizabeth Milne, theft of 15 sovereigns from Lazarus Myres, a Jewish travelling hawker in Aberdeen – 15 months imprisonment. Two men convicted of highway robbery outside Huntly – 14 years transportation.' It then details the trial of the men charged with organising and leading the Stonehaven riot. Witnesses were called but, as with all good trials involving mobbing and rioting, the evidence became blurred, if not completely contradictory. The ringleader, one Daniel Donald Davidson from Inverness, was variously described as striking the fatal blow and being simply a bystander. At one point, a witness even portrayed him as the man who had defended local men James Walker and John Carnegie from the mob.

Whatever the evidence, there was only one possible outcome and an example had to be made. Six men were accused of mobbing and rioting. Five received custodial sentences. The sixth, Daniel Davidson, was sentenced on 12 April 1848 to seven years penal servitude in Van Diemen's Land, better known today as Tasmania. Transported on the sailing ship *Nile II* alongside 299 fellow convicts, he reached his destination in October 1850, after a voyage lasting 109 days.

His great-great-granddaughter, Vicki Pearce, of Shearwater in modern-day Tasmania, has researched his story. She writes that:

Daniel Donald married Margaret Griffin 19 July 1853, at Bellerive, Tasmania. They lived at Kangaroo Point on the eastern shore … They had seven children and lived at Triabunna, on the East Coast of Tasmania. Daniel worked at the sandstone quarries. He was admitted to the General Hospital on 19 August 1874, suffering from pneumonia, and died on 31 August 1874.

The official penal record states that on the day of his demise, he was free by servitude, having spent twenty-four years in the colony, and that he was buried by friends. Daniel was but one of some 75,000 unfortunate convicts transported to Tasmania during the nineteenth century.

෨ ෨ ෨

The fishing port of Fraserburgh was the scene of another major riot in 1874. Following significant harbour investment, including the construction of a new breakwater, Fraserburgh had emerged as the Scottish herring capital, overtaking even Wick and Peterhead. Period photographs show the harbour filled with literally hundreds of fishing boats. Economic progress does not always come cheap, however, and the social effects of the annual influx of fishermen and their families from all over the North-east coast, plus a few thousand Heilanmen, could, on occasion, lead to law and order problems.

Billed in some circles as the 'Heilanmen's Great Riot of 1874', the events of 1 August that year stemmed, at least partly, from the fish curers' practice of paying not by the day, but by eight-week 'engagement'. One such pay day was known as the 'Heilanmen's foy', and on this day in 1874, the seasonal incomers received a substantial amount of money, which many began to invest short-term in the local brewing industry.

The Saturday evening started out well. However, as closing time approached, tempers became frayed and a Lewis man by the name of Buchanan began fighting with the locals. The affray soon became a riot and when the overwhelmed local police retreated to the town house they were repeatedly rushed by the drunken mob, who had wrongly assumed that their ringleader was under arrest within the building.

After much breaking of heads by police batons and an abortive and completely illegal attempt by local civilian volunteers to fire upon the mob, it began to rain heavily and the rioters quickly dispersed. Backed by armed Gordon Highlanders from Aberdeen, the next day the police began stopping and searching the Heilanmen. In particular, they examined heads for signs of baton wounds, leading local wags to nickname the Fraserburgh police as 'the phrenologists of the Bobby Brigade'. Several convictions were obtained in what may well have been the very last North-east riot during which the military were called out.

# S

## ⁂ SAMURAI ⁂

Variously known as 'the Scottish Samurai' or 'the Scot who shaped Japan', Thomas Blake Glover was born in Fraserburgh in 1838. His father worked as a coastguard officer and the family lived at various locations along the Aberdeenshire coastline, including Sandend, Collieston and Bridge of Don. On leaving school, Glover began work with the trading company Jardine, Matheson & Co. and quickly progressed to the Shanghai office before taking up a post in Japan.

His role in Shanghai has often been glossed over in order to present a popular image of Glover as an enlightened trader intent on hauling an impoverished Japan into the industrial age. In truth, however, Jardine Matheson & Co. were happy to trade in everything from silks and tea to guns and opium. Glover excelled in his role as trader and alongside making vast amounts of profit for his employer, he soon started taking a substantial cut for himself.

He moved to Japan, in 1859 aged 21, at a time when various rival clans were warring for control of the country. For more than 200 years, foreign trade with Japan had been permitted to the Dutch and Chinese exclusively. However, following an episode of gunboat diplomacy in 1853, the US government had forced the Japanese to open trade up to the West. Glover arrived in good time to use his proven skills to exploit the situation. Soon he was supplying both sides in the civil war with guns and munitions. Before long he was taking orders for the building of warships, to be built in Aberdeen, to arm a fledgling Japanese Navy.

The market for weaponry soon became saturated and he turned to mining to maintain his by now dwindling fortune. Demand for coal had surged as steamships began to proliferate in Japanese waters. In partnership with a Japanese clan, Glover invested in developing the Takashima coal mine on an island near Nagasaki in 1868. The mine was the first in the country to employ Western methods. Mitsubishi acquired the mine in 1881 in the organisation's first main diversification beyond shipping.

Glover is often credited with importing the first steam engine into Japan and being instrumental in the formation of the Mitsubishi conglomerate. Japan also lacked modern facilities for repairing ships, so Glover imported the necessary equipment to construct a dry dock in Nagasaki in 1868. He later sold his share to the government, which leased the dock to Mitsubishi as part of the shipyard in 1884. By 1905 Japan had, by many accounts, become the third largest naval power in the world.

There are many enduring myths surrounding the life and career of Thomas Blake Glover. One involves the notion that his Japanese wife Tsuru was somehow the inspiration for Puccini's opera 'Madame Butterfly'. There appears to be little substance to this idea. A booklet produced by Aberdeen City Council to publicise the area's links with Glover asserts that 'the association of Glover Garden in Nagasaki and Madame Butterfly no doubt relates to the fact that American soldiers after the Second World War dubbed the house Madame Butterfly House'.

Glover eventually became famous in Japan and was the first non-Japanese to be awarded the Order of the Rising Sun. When he died in Tokyo in 1911 aged 73, his ashes were interred in Nagasaki's Sakamoto International Cemetery. Fraserburgh Heritage Centre hosts a permanent exhibition celebrating Glover's North-east links and his former house in Nagasaki attracts 2 million visitors each year.

Alongside his warmongering business interests, Glover was a founding partner in what is now the Japanese Kirin Brewery. Each month local authorities in Nagasaki pay homage to their famous resident by placing a bouquet of flowers and a bottle of Kirin on his grave.

Until quite recently, the plaque on Glover's headstone advised visitors that he was an Englishman. Fortunately, the quirky error has now been rectified and the memorial now advises tourists of his undisputed Aberdeenshire heritage.

## ❧ STORMS ❧

July 2014 saw the crew of the Fraserburgh lifeboat summoned to rescue the crew of the fishing trawler *Sovereign*, which had run aground at Cairnbulg some nine years before.

A member of the lifeboat crew told reporters that a tourist had been standing on Tiger Hill when she spotted the ship lying on its side on a reef. Scottish television news reported that:

> She must have thought that it had just freshly sunk and made the call to the RNLI. It is a familiar landmark to locals but you can see how easy it would be for a visitor to mistake it for a vessel in distress. It was a mistake made with the best of intentions.

The Banff-registered trawler had in fact run aground during a storm in December 2005; the five fishermen on board being airlifted to safety. The rusting wreck later made international headlines when it made a surprise appearance on a promotional

The *Life of Pi* shipwreck at Cairbulg. (© Duncan Harley)

cinema poster for the Hollywood movie *Life of Pi*. The blockbuster, an adaptation of the Yann Martel novel of the same name, tells the story a 16-year-old Indian boy who becomes a castaway when the ship carrying him to America is wrecked in a violent storm. Oddly, perhaps, the young lad is then marooned on a lifeboat with a wild tiger for company.

Meanwhile, at Cairnbulg, the winter storms from the North Sea continue to batter the wreck of the *Sovereign* and with each successive storm the shipwreck moves closer and closer to the shore.

Local wags at Cairnbulg and the neighbouring village of Inverallochy, fearful perhaps of having a genuine tiger making it ashore to take up residence on Tiger Hill, are seemingly planning to erect a tiger enclosure in the village, just in case.

ⓒ ⓒ ⓒ

The village of Crovie is probably the best-preserved nineteenth-century fishing village in the North-east and is a place well used to storms. Indeed, for generations the locals have coped with everything the sea could throw at them and, until 1953, felt secure in the knowledge that they knew how to survive the fury of the winter storms.

In February 1903, they had risked life and limb to rescue the crew of the SS *Vigilant* when, following engine failure, it was driven ashore on the Rotten Beach just down from the village. Following a joint effort with the folk of nearby Gamrie, all six crew were rescued and there is now a memorial to the event on the beachfront.

The year 1953 began well for Crovie folk, with a few fine days and some light sleet. There was nothing unexpected, weather-wise, and the village was expecting a typical Scottish winter. Then, without warning, the January storms began in earnest. A full moon, low pressure over the North Sea, swelling tides and high winds combined to form a fatal situation that claimed lives and flooded thousands of homes on low-lying land all along the east coast and as far south as Holland.

Accompanied by a hurricane, the North Sea flood of 1953 was one of the most devastating natural disasters ever recorded in the United Kingdom. The forests of

Crovie. (© Duncan Harley)

Aberdeenshire had just begun to regenerate from the effects of two wars and were now flattened yet again by the gales.

The storm surge hit Crovie around midday on 31 January. Luckily, the fisher folk were wide awake and looking out to sea. Windows were shattered and roofs destroyed. Shutters made to withstand waves proved ineffective against the wind. Anything loose was swept away and the path along the Rotten Shore leading to Gardenstown was destroyed. The seawall and pier were badly damaged and the bridge over the burn swept away. Frightened villagers watched as giant waves surged over the roofs of the houses. As the storm raged, villagers feared for their lives and took to the high ground above the village. By the next day, the worst was past.

In the retelling, locals recalled the sight of Eider ducks in flooded kitchens and the smell of paraffin from the wrecked tank outside the flooded village shop. By some miracle, the fishing boats on the Greenie survived, but Crovie folk were apprehensive that it could happen again.

After the storm, many, including the local council, wondered if it was worth rebuilding the village. At a meeting in Banff, the county architect suggested that the place be abandoned. The future of Crovie seemed in doubt.

Wrecked houses were apparently sold for next to nothing. One is reported to have fetched a paltry £13. To this day locals assert that almost the entire village changed hands for 'jelly beans'. Crovie nowadays consists mainly of holiday lets and claims to be one of only two places in the world to be blessed with a north pole.

The Crovie North Pole is quite easy to reach and tourists are advised to simply walk to the far end of the village to the drying green beside the old mission hall. A metal clothes pole painted green marks the spot and helpfully has the words 'North Pole' painted on it. Visitors to the picturesque coastal village are strongly advised that 'if you don't walk around the North Pole, then you haven't "done" Crovie'.

## ⁎ TOILETS ⁎

The timber-built railway station at Ballater was at one time frequented by the royal family in the days when the journey north to Balmoral involved rail travel. When the Deeside line closed to passengers in 1966 the building found new use as shop units and even incorporated a tourist information centre and a restaurant. More recently, a part of the building was turned into a museum and visitors, if they were lucky, would stumble upon a mannequin dressed as Queen Victoria's loyal ghillie John Brown on the station platform. A second mannequin representing an ageing Victoria, complete with mourning dress, could be seen taking tea in the private royal apartments of the station building.

Those royal apartments, naturally, featured a royal loo. Thunder-box in form and with an ornately decorated porcelain pan, replete with acanthus leaves and brightly painted woodland flowers, the loo was off limits to ordinary travellers during Victoria's time. In more recent times, however, subject to an admission charge of course, the receptacle for the royal poo was open to the public gaze. However, after several visitors had succumbed to the allure of sitting on Victoria's throne and had used the device as intended by the manufacturers, VisitScotland was forced to add a cling-film cover as a deterrent.

When the station building burned to the ground in May 2015, the royal thunder-box perished in the blaze. There are plans to rebuild the station and eventually reopen an exact replica of the original building.

Meantime, visitors to Ballater can view Victoria's back-up royal loo at the Deeside Inn on Victoria Road. Based on the design of the royal waiting room at Sandringham, the royal throne room at the hotel lies partially hidden amongst period features such as wooden panelling and exposed-beam ceilings but staff are generally delighted to provide a guided tour of the 8ft square facility. A hotel spokesperson recently commented that 'we asked the royal protection squad to flush out any concerns regarding the authenticity of the loo and have concluded that it is the genuine article'.

Currently, however, a royal flush remains out of the question since the plumbing is distinctly Victorian.

The royal loo at Ballater station. (© Duncan Harley)

༄ ༄ ༄

David Ferguson's *Shipwrecks of North East Scotland* describes the Aberdeenshire coastline as 'a veritable trap for shipping' and lists over 200 known wreck locations. The wreck maps for the coastline between Stonehaven in the south and Portsoy in the north read like a who's who of international shipping. There are ships from every maritime nation on earth alongside countless German and British casualties from the two major conflicts of the twentieth century.

One such wreck is the German submarine *U-1206*. In 2012 a team of divers from Buchan came across the submerged wreck of a U-boat at a depth of 262ft some 12 miles off Cruden Bay. The wreck was said to be in very good condition despite the fact it had been on the seabed for around seventy years. The wreck had in fact already been discovered in the 1970s during survey work for the BP Forties Field oil pipeline to Cruden Bay, but documents recording her location were subsequently misplaced. The story of the sinking of this U-boat is a strange one. It was apparently sunk by a toilet malfunction.

*U-1206* went into service in March 1944 and was assigned to active duty under the command of Kapitänleutnant Karl-Adolf Schlitt. On 14 April 1945, just twenty-four days prior to the end of hostilities, the submarine was cruising underwater just off the Buchan coast when a crewmember, possibly the captain, answered a call of nature. Unfortunately, *U-1206* was fitted with a newly designed high-pressure underwater flushing toilet. Previously, crews regularly 'slopped-out' using buckets that were taken topside at the earliest opportunity and emptied into the sea. The new hi-tech system did away with this messy procedure and waste was passed through a series of valves before being fired at high pressure into the sea in the form of a sort of poop-torpedo.

But the system only worked safely at shallow depths and only crewmembers versed in the flushing procedure were authorised to operate the valves. The captain obviously hadn't read the manual and, as he attempted to flush the loo, something went badly wrong. A toilet specialist was summoned but misunderstood the situation and opened the wrong valve, resulting in seawater entering the boat.

Now, the submarine's battery compartment was situated directly underneath the toilet floor and when the incoming saltwater combined with the battery acid, toxic chlorine gas was produced. Things soon got out of hand. Forced to surface in order to vent the fumes, the submarine was quickly spotted and then, understandably, bombed by Allied aircraft, forcing the unfortunate Captain Schlitt to order the crew overboard before scuttling the vessel. One crewmember died in the air attack and several more drowned in the North Sea as they abandoned ship. Forty-six submariners made it to shore and spent the remaining weeks of the war in captivity.

In some ways, the surviving crew of *U-1206* were extremely lucky since the high attrition rate among U-boat crews meant that the average life expectancy of a crewman in 1945 was only sixty days. Perhaps instead of going down in history as the only U-boat ever to have been sunk by a toilet, the *U-1206* crewmembers should be remembered as the only submarine crew ever to have been saved by a toilet.

## ⁂ TYPHOID ⁂

The Aberdeen typhoid outbreak began quietly on 16 May 1964 when two university students were admitted to hospital suffering from 'pyrexia of unknown origin'. Further cases soon emerged and by the end of the epidemic 507 cases had been confirmed, including eighty-six children under the age of 12. There were three deaths plus an additional eight related cases treated elsewhere, including one in Canada.

By 17 June the epidemic was deemed officially over. A William Low supermarket in Aberdeen city centre was identified as the source of the epidemic and it was concluded that a 3kg can of Argentine corned beef had been the initial infective source. Argentine factories at the time routinely used untreated river water as a coolant in the canning process and suspicion focused on the possibility of contaminated water entering through burst can seams, causing bacterial contamination of the contents.

The news of the epidemic was reported widely around the globe with one Spanish periodical reporting that towns throughout Aberdeenshire were littered with rotting corpses waiting to be thrown into the sea.

In the wake of the outbreak, there were enquiries at both local and national level, the Milne Enquiry being perhaps the most influential. The Milne Report squarely placed the blame on imports from Argentina but bizarrely concluded that there was no evidence that the infected meat could have come from government stockpiles. This was an issue because government warehouses at the time held vast stocks of Argentine corned beef as part of a national emergency plan to tide the UK over in case of a nuclear war and each year around 10% of the stockpile was released into the domestic market.

It took almost ten years to dispose of the stockpiled emergency corned beef. The method of disposal chosen was to export the suspect meat with a proviso that it should be reprocessed. Not only had the unfortunate citizens of Aberdeenshire eaten the evidence from the initial source of the outbreak but unsuspecting citizens abroad would unwittingly consume the remaining evidence.

In a nod to the stereotypical notion that Aberdonians are careful with the contents of their wallets, a Scottish entertainer of the time added his brand of humour to the already large collection of derogatory comments surrounding the epidemic. That man was Andy Stewart, who should perhaps have known better. Infamously, he satirised not only the folk of Aberdeen but also the entire Scottish nation when he suggested that only in Aberdeen could 500 people each obtain a slice from a single can of corned beef. Despite the dark humour, almost 150,000 folk paid to attend his sell-out 1964 run at His Majesty's Theatre Aberdeen.

As a postscript, Michael Noble MP, then Secretary of State for Scotland, announced in September 1964 that in the light of the Aberdeenshire typhoid epidemic he would ensure that additional funding was made available to any local authority in Scotland 'wishing to provide hand washing facilities within public conveniences'. He urged that councils should take up this generous offer before the end of the financial year. Unbelievably, the vast majority of public toilets of the period had no such facilities!

North-eastern folk were, of course, already in the habit of washing their hands at every available opportunity despite comments by local comedy revue act 'Scotland the What' that 'we never washed wir' hands unless we did the lavvie first'.

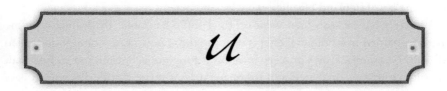

## ❖ UISGEBEATHA ❖

*Uisgebeatha* is an occasionally used Gaelic term for 'water of life'. Over time it has, according to some sources, been abbreviated and corrupted to form the word 'whisky'. Although much has been made of the two possible spellings 'whisky' and 'whiskey', many prefer to use the less contentious term 'scotch' to describe the golden nectar.

There are, of course, a great many references to scotch in both literature and poetry and Robert Burns was certainly a fan of a dram, as this extract from 'John Barleycorn' clearly illustrates:

> John Barleycorn was a hero bold,
> Of noble enterprise;
> For if you do but taste his blood,
> 'Twill make your courage rise.
>
> 'Twill make a man forget his woe;
> 'Twill heighten all his joy;
> 'Twill make the widow's heart to sing,
> Tho' the tear were in her eye.
>
> Then let us toast John Barleycorn,
> Each man a glass in hand;
> And may his great posterity
> Ne'er fail in old Scotland!

The Garioch town of Inverurie nowadays has few links to the distilling of scotch, but does boast a good few pubs and hotels that in their day would almost certainly have bottled their own blends. An Aberdeenshire business directory dating from the 1920s advertises the merits of the spirit suppliers of old. Alongside adverts proclaiming the merits of local hostelries, such as the Commercial Hotel and the Black Bull Inn, a full-page feature promoted the business of specialist family grocer

George Jackson, who advertised his whiskies as 'Pure, unblended Malt Whiskies from the best Highland Distilleries'.

Bizarrely, Mr Jackson then went on to claim: 'The public, by dealing with me are safeguarded from the evil effects of using those poisonous compounds called Blends.' George Jackson's grocery business is long gone, but interest in fine malt whisky continues unabated and there are at least seven distilleries within easy travelling distance of Inverurie. George Jackson would have approved.

໒໑ ໒໑ ໒໑

Chosen as a film location for the 2016 remake of the Ealing comedy *Whisky Galore!*, the historic coastal town of Portsoy has recently been referred to by publicists as 'The Village of the Drammed'. Quite what the author of the original novel *Whisky Galore*, Sir Compton Mackenzie, would have made of the casting of whimsical stand-up comedian Eddie Izzard as lead in the new film production is unclear. Additionally, by a strange coincidence, just as casting for the film began, London auctioneer Bonhams listed for sale a rare bottle of Glen Boyne Old Scotch Whisky. The sale catalogue indicates that the Glen Boyne may have been bottled in the back shop of Portsoy grocer G.G. McRobbie in the late nineteenth century. There is, however, some doubt regarding the provenance of the spirit since, although Portsoy had a distillery in Burnside Street during pre-railway days, this probably predates the Bonhams item. Whisky connoisseurs suspect that the Glen Boyne might actually have been distilled at nearby Glenglassaugh Distillery. The mystery remains unsolved and the half-filled bottle of scotch failed to meet the reserve at auction.

໒໑ ໒໑ ໒໑

The distillery at Banff suffered extensive damage due to a fire in May 1877 and, following the rebuilding of the plant, the owners retained a fire engine on the premises as a precautionary measure. However, the precaution was to no avail when in 1940, the Luftwaffe bombed Banff on at least two occasions.

The first attack was on the town's historic Duff House. Nowadays in the care of Historic Scotland, the building was constructed for William Duff, 1st Earl of Fife and completed in 1740 after five years of work. Built to a design by William Adam, the Georgian mansion has undergone many changes during the last century or so. From early beginnings as a stately home, it became a luxury hotel, then a sanatorium for the 'scientific treatment of disorders of nutrition excluding inebriation' and, briefly, a Second World War POW camp.

In 1939, Duff House was requisitioned by the War Office and, for a short time, housed German POWs. Tragically, at approximately 8.30 on the morning of 22 July 1940, a single German aircraft bombed the property, killing a British guard and seven German prisoners. The stonework on the frontage of the building still shows blast damage from the raid.

On 16 August 1941, another lone German raider bombed Banff Distillery but this time with less tragic results. Two bonded warehouses caught fire and, despite the best efforts of the distillery fire brigade, the buildings were destroyed, the contents variously going up in flames or running into a local burn.

Local lore has it that the fire fighters managed to salvage some of the whisky by scooping it up in their helmets and that the geese at nearby Old Manse Farm became quite inebriated when they drank the water from a whisky-laden pond.


## ⚜ UNDERWORLD ⚜

Hidden deep within the woods on the Crowmallie estate near Pitcaple is a massive statue of Persephone, daughter of Zeus and harvest goddess Demeter. Carved from millstone grit and weighing some 8.5 tons, the sculpture stands in a glade just west of the Pictish Maiden Stone. There is no accompanying plaque and information relating to the artwork is confusing to say the least.

Some locals claim that it was sculpted over the course of many years by the demented son of a local landowner who, in his saner moments, showed real artistic promise. Others attribute the work to a woman from nearby Drumdurno, a factoid that when checked seems unlikely since the woman in question would have been barely 9 years of age when the statue was completed.

In fact, the statue is the work of sculptor Sean Crampton and was commissioned by the landowner at Crowmallie around 1961. Born in 1918, Crampton first took up sculpture in the 1930s and studied at the Central College of Art in Birmingham. He enjoyed working with religious themes and his work can be found in many churches throughout the UK. Although his early leanings were towards silversmithing, he is most famous for his large welded bronze work, including the construction the Fourteen Stations of the Cross in the Church of St Edmonds.

Crampton's artistic career was interrupted by the Second World War and he served in both Italy and the Western Desert, reaching the rank of second lieutenant. While leading his men in Italy he was awarded the Military Cross for displaying 'Great gallantry and extremely high powers of leadership and devotion to duty.' It was 1944 and Crampton's platoon was out on reconnaissance duty. While crossing an Italian field, he suddenly felt the trigger of a landmine go off under his foot. 'Without hesitation,' reads the official report, 'Lieutenant Crampton shouted to those near him to get down while keeping his foot pressed on the mine, which went off under it.' It was a German S-mine, also known as a 'Bouncing Betty'. When triggered, these lethal devices launched themselves into the air before

Ben Harley and the statue of Persephone at Crowmallie. (© Duncan Harley)

detonating at chest level, spraying shrapnel in all directions. Crampton's lower leg was, of course, blown off by the explosion, but he and his men survived, probably due to his choice to keep his foot firmly on the mine, thus stopping it from springing up in the air.

So what has this got to do with Persephone? Well, in Greek mythology, Persephone was the daughter of Demeter, the goddess of the harvest. She was carried off by Hades, ruler of the underworld, to become his wife. However, Zeus, king of the gods, decreed that she could return on condition that she had eaten no food in the underworld. Sadly, since she had eaten the seeds of a pomegranate, she was only allowed to spend half of each year above ground. Despite the odds, she gained her freedom at least for a part of each year.

The visitor, on seeing Crampton's artwork at Crowmallie, might well wonder if the inspiration for the sculpture had something to do with his experience that fateful day in Italy when he beat the odds and survived certain death by defying the ruler of the underworld.

## ❖ VAMPIRES ❖

'Delighted with everything and everybody and hope to come again' reads an August 1884 entry in the guestbook of the Kilmarnock Arms Hotel at Cruden Bay. The signature alongside the entry reads 'Mr and Mrs Bram Stoker'. Stoker, author of the gothic vampire horror classic *Dracula*, and many other literary sensations, spent most of that August at the hotel with his wife and son.

He returned frequently over the subsequent twenty years and wrote at least part of *Dracula* at Crooked Lum Cottage, his holiday home at Cruden Bay. There is a strong local belief that his tale of Transylvanian terror was heavily influenced by nearby Slains Castle, although Ecclesgreig Castle at St Cyrus and the town of Whitby in Yorkshire also claim to be Stoker's inspiration.

However, visitors to Cruden Bay will rarely fail to sympathise with the view that Slains is indeed the genuine inspiration for Stoker's Gothic classic. Bram Stoker

Slains Castle. (© Duncan Harley)

described 'a vast ruined castle … whose broken battlements showed a jagged line against the moonlit sky'. He goes on: 'I saw the whole man slowly emerge from the window and began to crawl down the castle wall over that dreadful abyss, face down, with his cloak spreading around him like great wings.' Slains today is a roofless ruin perched high on a cliff top above the North Sea. Accessible only on foot, it is easy to imagine on approach that the howling winds screaming through the abandoned ruins are a portent of evil. Indeed, few visitors could fail to make the Dracula connection.

In 2012 an outline planning application was submitted to turn the Transylvanian ruin into holiday apartments. Locals were unhappy and turned to the local press for support. Amid lurid headlines such as 'Back from the dead holiday flats plan for Dracula Castle' and 'This development will drive a stake through the heart of a historic landmark', the scheme appears to have been put on hold. To date the castle, described by Bram Stocker as 'a vast ruined castle, from whose tall black windows came no ray of light', remains just that and most folk hope that it stays that way.

# ⁕ VITRIFICATION ⁕

Scattered across the Aberdeenshire hilltops are a series of vitrified forts dating back perhaps to the Iron Age. While archaeologists struggle to understand the method of construction, many oddball theories as to their origins abound. Supporters of the 'ancient astronauts theory' believe that the vitrified ruins provide irrefutable evidence that death rays created by superior extra-terrestrial beings were used in ancient times to melt granite to form the defensive structures. Others believe that the fusion of solid rock was caused by bonfires lit as part of a religious ceremony or, alternatively, that fierce attacks by enemy tribes resulted in huge fires that caused the very rocks to melt.

Detractors consider it unlikely that the hilltop forts at Dunnideer or Tap o' Noth could burn long enough to melt rock, commenting that this would have been 'as near as the European Iron Age got to Las Vegas lit against the Nevada desert'. In an attempt to solve the mystery, a full-scale combustible model fort was constructed on a council rubbish tip at Tullos Hill in 1980. Financed by Yorkshire Television, the building and subsequent ignition of the wall was to be aired as part of the *Arthur C. Clarke's Mysterious World* science fiction series due for broadcast in the autumn of that year.

Measuring a massive 29½ft in length by 13m wide, the 10ft high structure resembled a funeral pyre fit for a giant. On the appointed day, and with the addition of an entire articulated lorry load of timber offcuts, the conflagration began. As the core temperature rose to a heady 800°C, hopes were high that fusion would take place and to aid this, a lorry load of mattresses was added to the bonfire. Whether the ancients would have had access to such items was apparently not an experimental issue.

After twenty-two hours, scientists began sifting through the embers looking for vitrified material. This proved difficult since not only was the structure still smouldering and liable to collapse, but the rubber-soled boots worn by the crew melted due to the heat. By 4 p.m. on 2 April, some forty-eight hours after the experiment had begun, the remains were bulldozed flat and the hunt began for vitrified rock.

In absolute terms, the resulting 6½lb of vitrified material located in the ashes was disappointing and the experimental report makes various claims explaining away the poor results. The newness of the wall, the lack of suitable hardwoods and the dampness of the firewood were highlighted, along with the tight TV production schedule. Critics of the time, who pointed out that perhaps the ancients had also suffered from damp firewood, were largely ignored. This was, after all, a sponsored experiment due to be aired on prime-time TV.

The vitrified stone produced in the Yorkshire Television experiment was eventually deposited at the University of Aberdeen's Anthropological Museum. Presumably the material is accompanied by an apologetic note explaining that but for some unexpected overnight drizzle there would have been much more vitrified rock available for display.

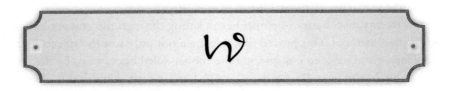

## ❖ WINDMILLS ❖

Many North-east folk were bemused when, in 2012, a full-page advertisement appeared in regional newspapers featuring an image of a Californian wind farm set next to a photo of the then First Minister Mr Alex Salmond, the suggestion being that two were in some way linked. The accompanying text also appeared to link the Lockerbie terrorist bombing with the Scottish government's policy on renewable energy and posed the question 'Is this the future for Scotland?'

Readers were urged to 'Take action. Write, demonstrate and protest Alex Salmond'. Some suspected that a left-wing anti-capitalist group might be behind the advertising campaign while others quietly assumed that 1 April had come early. However, on close inspection, tucked away in a corner of the page was an acknowledgement that the advert had been placed by a local Aberdeenshire golf course. Trump International Golf Links Scotland no less!

Aberdeen's *The Press and Journal*, one of the newspapers to publish the advert, carried a follow-up news item the following day headed 'Trump's turbines link to Lockerbie sick', and the Trump Organisation's former vice president George Sorial was quoted as saying that he had 'wanted the content' of the advert 'to be much stronger because Scotland is facing an economic and environmental meltdown if wind turbines are not stopped'.

As controversy surrounding the advert continued to mount, it emerged that the focus of debate was a £230 million offshore wind farm development, due to be sited just north of Aberdeen and in full view of Trump International Golf Links at Balmedie. Indeed, at one point Donald Trump was quoted as having said that: 'We will spend whatever monies are necessary to see to it that these huge and unsightly industrial wind turbines are never constructed.' The Advertising Standards Authority quickly intervened following a number of complaints and ruled that the advertising materials 'breached the rules on grounds of misleading advertising and substantiation and should not appear again in their present form'.

Even Don Quixote would have been hard put to make sense of it all.

∽ ∽ ∽

Controversy over wind power is nothing new, as the story of Abercrombie's windmill illustrates.

At first glance, the Glassaugh windmill can easily be mistaken for a Pictish Broch or even a Martello tower, and is known as 'the Cup and Saucer' because of its distinctive shape. Set back over 500m from the A98 between Portsoy and Banff, the structure has a covering of ivy that masks the outline of the building and suggests a ruined tower house with a walled garden encircling the base. Nothing could be further from the truth however!

In common with much of the Banff and Buchan coastline, the area around Portsoy is full of Pictish remains. These are often built over or indeed incorporated into later structures such as farm houses, churches and dykes. The Glassaugh windmill is just such a building.

General James Abercrombie of Glassaugh was, as his title suggests, a military man. He was born in 1706 to a wealthy Banffshire family and, as was the custom of the time, he purchased a major's commission to enter the army in 1742. He was promoted to colonel in 1746 and major general in 1756. The general is credited with having particularly good organisational skills but very little understanding of the art of warfare. In fact, he was known to his troops as 'Mrs Nanny Abercrombie' because of his provision of tents and hot food on the long marches through North America during the French and Indian War of 1754–1763.

Abercrombie's windmill. (© Duncan Harley)

Unfortunately, in July 1758 he met his 'Charge of the Light Brigade' moment when he quite rashly directed his troops to make a frontal assault on a fortified French position without the benefit of artillery support. More than 2,000 of his force of 15,000 were killed or wounded, resulting in the good general being recalled to Britain, where he duly became a Member of Parliament in a government committed to supporting the cause of British dominion over the Northern Territories of America and Canada. No surprises so far, then.

When Major General Abercrombie MP returned to his native Scotland, he took over the running of the family estate at Glassaugh and, possibly lacking much to do in the Parliament of the day, he began organising the improvement of the agricultural economy of the estate.

This was a time of land improvement and land enclosure. Labour was plentiful and cheap as a large number of Irish Catholics had been dispossessed by the influx of English and Scottish aristocracy and had sought work on the land in Scotland. What was Major General Abercrombie MP to do? He had been a poor general indeed but, as has been said, he had good organisational skills. In the true spirit of Jaroslav Hašek's *Good Soldier Švejk*, which is essentially a series of absurdly comic episodes, Abercrombie decided to build a giant windmill.

Now, in those far-off days, the majority of mills were powered by water. There are tens of thousands of watermills in the UK and, at a guess, there must be at least one in every inhabited town and village in Aberdeenshire. Transport was improving during the 1750s but local grain mills were still the order of the day. Windmills were not unknown in the North-east, but were not common due to the ease and availability of water power. The good general, however, decided that wind was the way to go.

As any engineer will know, the biggest challenge in building large structures is the sourcing of construction materials. If you need to build a wall then you will require large quantities of heavy and difficult-to-transport stone. The shorter the journey from quarry to building site the better. Fortunately, Abercrombie had a ready supply of building materials in the form of a Bronze Age burial cairn. The folk who had built the cairn would have no objections to its recycling after all and, of course, at that time there was no legislation in force to protect the ancient structure.

The Cup and Saucer was born. Using the materials from the ancient cairn, Abercrombie bade his workers build an enormous four-storey windmill complete with a tapering tower topped with white sails. It must have been the sight of the century for folk who had never travelled further than Sandend or Portsoy.

How long Abercrombie's windmill was in full tilt is not recorded, but in a letter dated 23 August 1761, the good general advised his eldest daughter that high winds had almost blown off 'the pompon of the wind mill which was only set up yesterday'. The ivy-covered granite stump of the structure is all that remains today to remind us of the man who had the vision to build it all those years ago.

In a 1979 article, local Portsoy historian Mary Mackie describes an old painting of nearby Glassaugh House that clearly shows an image of the Glassaugh windmill in full sail. She also suggests that the path connecting the nearby Glenglassaugh Distillery passed through the windmill by the north and south arches, thus linking the windmill to a nearby public house known as the Black Jug.

So there we have it. The windmill known locally as the Cup and Saucer also has a milk jug.

## ⁂ WORSHIP ⁂

Perhaps not quite on a par with the Italian chapel in Orkney, the cramped attic space of writer, artist and sometime priest Peter Anson's house at No. 2 Low Shore Macduff attracted national interest when the *Sunday Express* gave it nationwide publicity in 1946, after its first mass was celebrated.

In the attic of this cramped fisherman's cottage, Peter had created a small chapel that, at the time, was the only Catholic place of worship in the entire town. Peter's home had already become an open house for visiting seamen and was a gathering place for many youngsters in the town. Affectionately known as 'Harbour Head' in his writings, it was to be Peter's home for fifteen years.

The oratory, dedicated to Our Lady of the Ships and St Peter the Fisherman, was for many years also the only chapel on the Scottish mainland dedicated to the spiritual needs of mariners. Harbour Head's loft chapel sported an altar made by local joiner Geordie Watt and a canvas altar cover sewn from rough sail cloth by Jim Blair, the local sailmaker. On leaving Macduff in 1952, Anson dismantled the oratory and shipped the contents to France for reuse by the Mission de la Mer.

There are no traces now of either Peter's house or the loft chapel at Harbour Head. The building later served as a net store before eventually being demolished to make way for harbour improvements, leaving both Macduff and Aberdeenshire much the poorer.

෨ ෨ ෨

Visitors to Buckie often remark upon the number of churches in the town. Recently, a TripAdvisor reviewer commented that 'the most amazing thing about the town is the number of churches and the comparatively small number of pubs'.

Fishing communities traditionally have a strong religious leaning, but few towns of Buckie's size offer such a broad degree of religious diversification. Many of the local churches are architecturally stunning and the twin-towered, red sandstone St Peter's in St Andrew's Square must be one of the grandest churches in the whole of Scotland. Originally conceived as a cathedral for the Roman Catholic Diocese of Aberdeen, St Peter's opened for business in 1857, to the alarm of some folk who referred to the twin spires, visible many miles out to sea, as 'Yon twa horns o the Deil!' Kinder folk referred to the building as the 'Cathedral of the North'.

❧ ❧ ❧

In post-Reformation eighteenth-century Aberdeenshire, the celebration of mass was banned and the practising of Catholicism often involved secretive worship. In consequence, church services often took place in secret and in buildings that blended easily into the landscape.

The small Roman Catholic Church of St Ninian's at Tynet near Buckie is just such a building and, in stark contrast to the open grandeur of Buckie's St Peter's, St Ninian's makes no pretence whatsoever to architectural greatness. Built around 1755 and enlarged in 1787, the church remains open for worship and closely resembles a long stone-built barn. Few would give it a second glance.

Known as the 'Banffshire Bethlehem', St Ninian's is probably the oldest Scottish post-Reformation chapel available for worship today. Alongside the 'clandestine' congregation at Tynet, Buckie is also home to Methodist, Baptist, Church of Scotland, Gospel Hall Brethren, Episcopal and Salvation Army congregations.

❧ ❧ ❧

St Ninian's Roman Catholic church at Tynet. (Courtesy of Janice Rayne)

St Margaret's church in Huntly is built in a style reminiscent of the churches and cathedrals more often found in Spain. Described by author Peter Anson as 'a curious octagonal shaped building unlike any church I have ever seen ... it was the first Catholic Chapel in Scotland to be provided with a bell since the Reformation. What a sensation it must have caused when that bell rang out for the first Mass.'

Funds for the construction were provided by John Gordon of Wardhouse near Insch. Gordon was then living in Cádiz, a fact that undoubtedly influenced the Spanish-inspired structure with its magnificent baroque tower. Completed in 1834, St Margaret's underwent complete restoration in 1990 with funding from the Scottish Heritage Trust. The main contractor Doric Construction was awarded the quirkily titled 'Plasterer's Trophy' in recognition of its high-quality workmanship.

The call to worship more often than not involves both the church bell and the church clock. However, even ecclesiastical timepieces can at times be a source of confusion, as the clock tower of the former parish church in Portsoy graphically illustrates. Three faces of the clock conform to the generally accepted practice of counting the hours in a one-to-twelve sequence, but the north-facing clock dial unaccountably has no nine and, confusingly, offers the viewer a choice of elevens.

Church clock errors are not uncommon however. The clock at St Mary Magdalene's in East Yorkshire bears Roman numerals up to thirteen instead of the more usual twelve, and Crimond church near Fraserburgh sports a timepiece with an extra minute between the numerals eleven and twelve, resulting in a 61-minute hour.

Local investigation regarding the Portsoy clock face's two elevens and missing nine led one resident to comment, 'It's about time someone did something about this.'

## ✥ X-RAYS ✥

When novelist and playwright Somerset Maugham published his short story 'Sanatorium' in 1928, few residents in the Deeside town of Banchory would have been in much doubt about the identity of the central character, Ashenden.

Ashenden relates a tale about a secret agent by the name of Major John Templeton who is slowly dying of pulmonary tuberculosis in a Scottish sanatorium. The plot owes its origins to Maugham's own experiences, both as a spy and as a patient at a Nordrach-on-Dee Sanatorium on the outskirts of Banchory. Ashenden is, of course, Somerset Maugham.

Maugham had been working for British Intelligence in a covert effort to stem the outbreak of the Russian Revolution. While stationed in Petrograd, during early 1917, he famously caught what he was to call 'a touch of tuberculosis'.

Nordrach-on-Dee Sanatorium at Banchory. (© Duncan Harley)

A lung specialist recommended a curative stay in a sanatorium and, in November 1917, Somerset Maugham booked himself into the Nordrach-on-Dee Sanatorium. He remained there as a patient until the spring of 1918, by which time he had completed the 'Sanatorium' story and also written the play *Home and Beauty*. Following a second stay, during the winter of 1918–19, Maugham was discharged with a clean bill of health.

Nowadays, the timber-built sanatorium is better known as Glen o' Dee Hospital. Founded as a private residential clinic for the treatment of tuberculosis, the facility opened on Christmas Eve 1900, offering treatment for up to fifty wealthy private patients. There were various treatments available, including X-ray therapy, which formed part of a curative system developed by Dr Otto Walther in the Black Forest region of Germany. The Nordrach regime, as it was called, involved a combination of fresh forest air, complete rest and a punishing 'overfeeding' diet involving intake of up to 9lb of food each day. The Banchory sanatorium was one of the first Nordrach sanatoriums to use X-rays in the diagnosis and treatment of TB and had its own laboratory and X-ray department.

As the incidence of tuberculosis declined during the 1920s, patient numbers declined also, and in 1928 the Nordrach-on-Dee building became first a fashionable hotel and then a military hospital. The building was briefly pressed into service as an overflow hospital during the 1964 Aberdeen typhoid outbreak. Latterly, the building provided care for the elderly before its eventual closure in 1998. The historic building was finally destroyed by fire in October 2016. Police treated the incident as wilful fire raising.

Ironically, the original Black Forest Nordrach design embodied the concept that timber-built sanatoria could, if necessary, be incinerated as a means of disposal at the end of their useful life as a means to eradicate any remaining vestige of disease within the structure.

## ❧ YTHAN ❧

The River Ythan, besides having the largest estuary on the Aberdeenshire coast, is a haven for wildlife including otters, wildfowl and perhaps even freshwater mussels. In past centuries, there was unrelenting commercial exploitation of Scottish freshwater pearl mussels and the creatures, which can live for 100 years and are protected by the Nature Conservation (Scotland) Act 2014, remain under threat of extinction across the entire Scottish river network.

The Roman biographer Suetonius wrote that Caesar's admiration of these mussels' pearls was one of the many reasons for the Roman invasion of Britain in August of 55 BC and the Roman camp at Ythanwells probably offered the invaders access to both good potable water and to the River Ythan pearl fisheries.

Twelfth-century Scottish monarch Alexander I, King of Scots, was said to have the best pearl collection of any man living, and the Scottish crown jewels include seven large freshwater pearls, including one seemingly found in the early seventeenth century, in the Kelly Burn, a tributary of the Ythan.

In more recent years, the seal colony at the Ythan Estuary has become a favourite place for seal watching. Among the 2,000 animals that make up the Ythan colony is an adult female nicknamed 'Frisbee'. First spotted in 2015, she has what wildlife experts at first believed was an orange frisbee around her neck. This later turned out to be the remnants of a discarded collapsible dog bowl. Volunteers from the Ythan Seal Watch are hopeful that they can remove the offending article but refused to comment on local rumours that the afflicted seal would then be renamed 'Barker'.

Of the dozen or so crossing points that served the folk of Buchan up until the establishment of bridges over the Ythan, the ford at Ellon was one of the busiest and the growth and prosperity of the town is intimately connected with the river. Second only to the crossing point at Tanglandford near Tarves, which on occasion saw up to 10,000 cattle crossing in a single day, the Ellon crossing was a mere 39ft above sea level and offered the lowest fording point on the river.

The ford was superseded by a bridge in 1793 but by the 1920s the Auld Brig over the Ythan at Ellon was in urgent need of replacement. With a roadway a mere 16ft wide, it was unsuited to the needs of modern motor transport. Retained as a pedestrian bridge running alongside the modern road bridge, the Auld Brig was completed in 1793 after two years of construction. It remains the last-surviving example of the work of Banff mason James Robertson, being similar in design to his long-demolished bridge over the Don at Inverurie.

Records held by the Royal Commission on the Ancient and Historical Monuments of Scotland indicate that following Robertson's completion of the Inverurie bridge, in 1791, the timber shuttering used to form the bridge arches was floated down the River Don, towed north by sea to Newburgh, then floated up the River Ythan for reuse in the construction of Ellon's Auld Brig.

The very last recorded ferry over the Ythan was operated by Tom Pirie. Better known locally as 'Boatie Tam', Mr Pirie, who died in 1992, for much of his life operated a small rowing boat to ferry people across the Ythan at Ellon's Waterford Dock. Tam was the last in a long line of Piries who operated the ferry, having inherited it from his mother, 'Boatie Mary', in the mid-twentieth century.

## ❖ YAWLS ❖

In February 2015, the Royal Mail published a commemorative stamp set entitled 'Working Sail', featuring the work of so-called 'pier head painters'. Working at speed in order to deliver finished ship portraits before the subject left port, pier head painters, such as Aberdeen fish porter Alexander Harwood (1873–1943), produced literally hundreds of paintings of North-eastern fishing vessels, including the *Herring Drifter Briar*, which features in the Royal Mail commemorative set.

The tradition continues to this day in the work of Lewis-based marine artist Margaret Maclean, who was recently commissioned to paint a portrait of the yawl *Northern Light*, a 75ft Zulu-class herring drifter owned and operated in the late nineteenth century by North Sea fisherman Daniel Sutherland, better known locally as 'Junties Dan'. Often described as the noblest sailing craft ever designed, Zulus became popular along the entire Aberdeenshire coastline towards the end of the nineteenth century and well into the twentieth, when many were converted to motor power. The Scottish Fisheries Museum at Anstruther has a full-size dry-berthed example of a Zulu drifter on permanent display. Carrying large sails on masts up to 60ft in height, these were fast boats, capable of around 12 knots and quite able to outrun the more modern coal-fired steam drifters that gradually took over from them.

The origins of the Zulu are slightly unclear and both William Campbell of Lossiemouth and W.G. Stephen of Banff are credited with the original design. In the 1870s, driven by the need to fish in more distant waters, a demand for fast, powerful, sail-driven boats emerged and Campbell's groundbreaking design fitted the bill. First built by Alexander Wood of Lossiemouth in 1879, the new boat

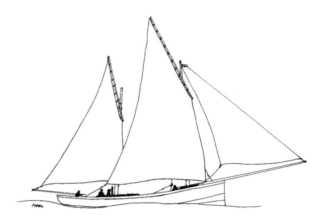

A Zulu drifter. (Courtesy of Margaret Maclean)

combined the best features from two existing successful fishing boat designs: the steeply raking stern of the 'Scaffie' and the vertical stem of the 'Fifie'. The result was a fast and highly manoeuvrable hybrid.

The Zulu boats were often built using the carvel method of planking, which was much stronger than the clinker system and, although they were two-masted, the boats carried three sails – a fore, a mizzen and a jib. The sails were heavy and difficult to haul when wet. The introduction of steam capstans eventually solved this problem and one of the very best capstan designs was engineered by MacDonald Brothers of Portsoy in the early 1900s.

Quite why William Campbell decided to call his new design 'Zulu' is unclear, but the Zulu wars were in full swing at the time and there were many North-eastern men fighting and dying in the Zulu kingdom. News of both military disasters and victories regularly featured in the local press and perhaps inspired Campbell to name his yawl after the Zulu warriors of King Cetshwayo.

A much more romantic version of the origins of the Zulu features a marriage between a Lossiemouth fisherman and a fisherwoman from Peterhead. On deciding to commission a new boat, they failed to agree on the final design. The husband had always sailed in a boat of the Fifie class and naturally wanted to build one after this design, but the wife's family were used to the Scaffie and she quite obstinately insisted on the latter type, rightly pointing out that she was, after all, providing half of the funds for the new craft.

After much discussion, a compromise was reached. The newly-weds agreed to combine the two designs: the husband got his way as regards the bow, and the wife got her way as regards the stern. The new design of yawl was duly built and christened *Nonesuch*, due to being neither one nor the other.

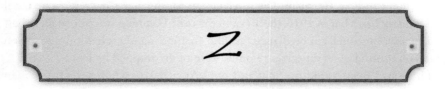

## ❧ ZEPPELINS ❧

During the First World War, the inhabitants of Peterhead became quite used to the sight of airships, from the nearby Royal Naval Air Station at Lenabo, overflying the town. Nicknamed 'gasbags' by the 1,500 or so naval personnel on the base, and 'Lenabo Soos', or flying pigs, by the townsfolk, these early airships often suffered mechanical breakdown.

In 1917, for example, a North Sea–class airship got into difficulties over Peterhead. Experiencing engine failure and forced to expel highly flammable gas to lose height, the 300ft long machine came into contact with the weathercock on the top of the town house, which ripped a hole in the fabric. Fortunately, the craft was only lightly damaged and the crew managed to land on the harbour's Smith Embankment, where crowds of spectators clung on to the mooring ropes until a few lorry loads of naval ratings arrived from the nearby airbase to take over.

Towards the end of the war, tragedy struck when a Lenabo-based airship was lost with all hands on patrol over the North Sea. There was speculation at the time that it had been shot down by a German U-boat but, given the poor safety record of these early airships, it is just as likely that the ungainly machine had simply crashed into the sea. A wooden propeller from the wreck eventually floated ashore and is now on display alongside a memorial plaque dedicated to the lost crew at St John's church, Longside.

Ꮿ Ꮿ Ꮿ

An airship of a quite different kind spread fear and panic across the Aberdeenshire countryside in 1916. The editions of both the *Aberdeen Free Press* and the *Aberdeen Daily Journal* for Thursday, 4 May 1916 carried the news that the war had finally arrived on Aberdeenshire's doorstep in the form of aerial bombing by a German zeppelin on the night of 2 May.

The headlines screamed 'Terrific Noise of Crashing Bombs' and 'Zeppelin at Rattray Head' with descriptions of up to seventeen bombs having been dropped over the North-east in the course of the attack. Zeppelin raids were common over southern England and on the Continent but it had been assumed that North-eastern Scotland was well out of range of raiders, whose bases were around twelve hours' flight away in Germany. The usual targets for the German crews were naval and military bases but in 1916, the art of night-time bombing was uncertain at best and many bombs fell on civilian areas. The airships mainly relied on navigation based on ground observation and bombs were often dropped by hand.

There had been a raid on Scotland on 2 April 1916, when several German airships bombarded Edinburgh's Grassmarket and a bonded warehouse at Leith, killing thirteen people on the ground. A plaque at Edinburgh Castle records the event.

A bomb fragment from the 1916 Zeppelin raid. (© Duncan Harley

Exactly one month later, the raiders returned. The intended targets this time were the Forth Rail Bridge and the naval base at Rosyth, but the navigation was faulty and only two of the eight hydrogen-filled airships, the L14 and the L20, even managed to locate mainland Scotland, never mind find the Forth Bridge.

In a farcical series of events, Zeppelin L14 mistook the Firth of Tay for the Firth of Forth and eventually dumped its bombs over Lunan Bay, near Montrose, injuring a horse. The 600ft-long L20 lumbered confidently north at a steady 45mph, possibly intending to bomb a secondary target of Royal Navy warships in the Cromarty Firth, before heading out to sea over Buchan's Rattray Head. Wildly off course and completely disorientated, the L20's sixteen-strong crew flew inland, bombing Craig Castle at Lumsden before overflying Kintore, Old Rayne and Insch, where they dropped bombs and a flare on a field at Hill of Flinder Farm. Mill of Knockenbaird and nearby Freefield House were also targeted. Amazingly though, there were no casualties and, next day, curious locals went in search of souvenirs in the form of bomb fragments.

In the aftermath, the *Aberdeen Free Press* ran a heavily censored feature article telling readers of 'Bombs Dropped in Fields … some windows in a mansion house and a cotter house broken by the concussion … no person sustained even the slightest injury.' The L20 eventually headed out over the North Sea to ask for directions, via loudhailer, from the startled crew of a fishing trawler, before heading over to Norway, where it ran out of fuel just off the Norwegian coast at Sandnes on 3 May. The Press Association reported that:

> Zeppelin L20 was reported this morning at 10 o'clock over the Southern part of the Jaederin coast. The aircraft flew slowly towards the north and came nearer and nearer to the coast, which it eventually crossed. It then passed at a low altitude over the country as far as Halsfirth where it came down in the water. The Zeppelin appears to have been damaged and it is reported that the crew jumped out of the gondolas into the sea near Hinna.

The German crew survived to fight another day but the L20 met a fiery end when a Norwegian Army officer set the wreck aflame with a well-placed shot from his flare pistol, thus ending this truly bizarre episode in the history of early aerial warfare.

## About the Author

Although not born and bred in Aberdeenshire, Duncan Harley considers the county his adoptive home. Early days penning letters and occasional impassioned articles to local newspapers gave way to a short career in local government, where his writing skills were honed. After various spells of self-employment, he worked for a time at a well-known street newspaper before eventually turning to freelance writing. Feature writing now takes up much of his time alongside the penning of both theatrical and literary reviews.

Duncan lives in rural Aberdeenshire with his cat Lucy and is surrounded by a huge pile of other people's books. At weekends and holidays, he and partner Janice like nothing better than to explore the history and landscape of the North-east.